Waiting...

In The Age of Instant Everything

By Rick Brown

Also by the Author

Call Me Al (a novel, available on Amazon, 2024)

Note to Readers

This book is intended to inspire thoughtful reflection and provide lighthearted perspectives on the concept of waiting. The ideas shared are meant for informational and entertainment purposes and should not be taken as definitive advice. The author and publisher disclaim any liability for actions taken based on the information in this book.

Copyright © 2025 by Rick Brown

First edition March 2025

ISBN 979-8-9927888-0-8

Dedication

To my wife, Kelly, who somehow endures my endless ramblings about waiting—even when she's the one waiting for me to finish a sentence. The best waiting moment of my life happened years ago at my favorite bar, The Irish Times. I was there with my buddy Jacek, waiting for him to return from the restroom, when I glanced across the room—and saw you. I may have been waiting for someone else, but fate had other plans. In that moment, I found forever. I love you, and I am beyond lucky that you keep waiting for me.

To Meghan, Lily, and TJ—each brilliant, kind, and endlessly inspiring in your own ways. You ground me, challenge me, and remind me to savor the pause. I am beyond proud of you.

In loving memory of my mom, whose kindness filled the moments in between—the small, quiet spaces where life truly happens. And to my dad, whose humor and warmth can brighten a stranger's day—and even inspire a book about waiting.

You all keep me laughing, grounded, and inspired—sometimes all at once. I love you more than words (or waiting) can express.

The Parable of the Cloudy Water

An old Zen master took his pupils to a quiet pond and stirred the water with a stick until it became cloudy with mud.

"Make the water clear again," he instructed them.

The students hurried to scoop, filter, and even blow on the water, but their efforts only made it worse. Frustrated, they turned to the master for guidance.

He smiled and said, "Stop. Just leave it be."

The students stood still, watching the water settle. Slowly, the mud sank to the bottom, and the pond became clear once more.

The master said, "Some things resolve themselves when you allow them the time to do so. Patience reveals clarity."

Part I

From Rocks to Clocks
A History of Human Delays

From Seed to Fruit:
History of Human Beings

Chapter One

Tick Tock: The Time Thief & The Birth of the Queue

"(Tick, tock) doo, doo, doo-doo Time keeps on slippin', slippin', slippin'... into the future."
– Steve Miller Band, Fly Like an Eagle
(A poetic way of saying, congrats, you've been on hold for 47 minutes.)

"Your call is very important to us. Please continue to hold…"

That robotic voice is lying. Your call is *not* important to them. You know it. They know it. And yet, here you are, trapped in hold music hell, slowly morphing into a sentient sigh while a tinny saxophone loops for the fifteenth time.

Waiting. It's the tax we all pay just for existing.

Think about it: You wake up, groggy, in desperate need of coffee. But first, you wait for the machine to drip at glacial speed. You jump in the shower—wait for the water to heat up. Get dressed—wait for the traffic lights to change. Crawl through a commute, only to arrive at work and wait for an elevator. Then, just as you settle into your desk, take your first glorious sip of coffee, and check your inbox—boom. The email you've been waiting for.

It's from your boss. Wait for it... asking you to wait for a follow-up email.

No matter how much progress we make, no matter how fast technology moves, waiting never actually disappears. It just mutates, taking new forms, sneaking into our lives in ways we barely notice. And that's the real scam: waiting doesn't hit us all at once. It drains us in tiny, forgettable increments—five minutes here, twenty minutes there—until one day, you wake up and realize you've spent *years* of your life in some mind-numbing cosmic void.

That's not an exaggeration. Studies suggest that, on average, we spend two to four years of our lives waiting. That's up to 1,460 days standing in lines, watching loading screens, trapped in traffic, listening to hold music that, let's be honest, might be a government experiment in psychological warfare. If you dedicated that time to actual study, you could earn a *bachelor's degree in waiting*—majoring in checkout lines, with a minor in stalled traffic.

And here's the real gut punch: Time is the one resource we can never get back. Money lost can be re-earned. Opportunities missed have a way of circling back. But time? Once it's gone, it's gone. If someone reached into your bank account every morning and took enough cash to buy a nice meal or a full tank of gas, you'd take action. But when time is stolen from us in small, relentless doses? We shrug and accept it.

But what if we didn't?

What if, instead of treating waiting as dead space—a glitch in the matrix where nothing happens but you still have to be there—we flipped the script? What if waiting wasn't a waste, but an opportunity?

That's what this book is about.

We're going to crack open the history of waiting, from ancient times to the industrial age to the buffering screens of today. We'll dig into the psychology of why time slows to a crawl in a DMV line but vanishes when you're binging a show. We'll look at who waits the longest (and surprise, it's not the 1%) and how corporations trick us into *loving* the very thing we claim to hate. And, most importantly, we'll uncover ways to make waiting *work for us*—because if we have to spend years of our lives in line, we might as well make it worth the time.

So buckle up—no, scratch that. You've already waited too long for a book like this. Let's get moving.

Before we dive into solutions, though, we need to take a close look at how we got here. As modern as our waiting frustrations feel, we're not the first generation to wrestle with them. First, we're going to take a trip back—way back—and explore the history of waiting. You'll see that for all our gripes about traffic jams and buffering streams, we've got nothing on the lengths people in history had to go just to endure the inevitable delays of life. Waiting isn't a new problem, but understanding how far we've come might just put things into perspective—and maybe even make you grateful for that slow-loading webpage.

Waiting isn't new—it just used to be a lot…slooooower.

Back When Everything Was Now

There was a time, long ago, before the wheel. Before fire. Back when life was one big Now. There was no word for *waiting*. Why would there be? Everything was happening or it wasn't.

You sat by the river, hoping the fish would swim by. You poked a rock, wondering if it would do something interesting. You grunted at the clouds because you *could*. And if someone asked, "Hey, what are you doing?" the only logical response would've been: *"Unngh."* Which meant nothing. And everything.

(Some linguists argue *"unngh"* is actually the earliest known precursor to "ugh," the modern-day sound we make while waiting in line at the DMV.)

It's fun to imagine when waiting was first *discovered*. Did some early human try to organize something for the first time? "We meet here. At sun-up. To hunt mammoth." Did his buddies show up late and, frustrated, he invented waiting? Or perhaps the realization hit more subtly:

> "Gruk said mammoth here. Mammoth not here."
>
> "Then we *unngh*?"
>
> "Yes. We *unngh*. Forever."

This might've been when the first clock was born—Gruk staring at the sky, noticing the sun creeping across the horizon while he muttered to himself, "When is now *not* enough anymore?"

The Word Wait

Of course, as waiting became more common, people needed a way to complain about it.

Enter: language.

Interestingly, the word *wait* comes from the Old North French *waitier*, which meant "to watch with hostile intent." Before that, it traces back to the Old High German *wahta*, meaning "a watch or a guard." Which makes sense: waiting wasn't passive—it was vigilance. Early waiting meant keeping one eye on the mammoth, the enemy, or the weather, because your life probably depended on it.

Funny to think: we started out waiting with such urgency and purpose, and now we're just staring at loading screens, sighing, *"Ugh."*

Waiting in Ancient Times

It is a truth universally ignored that the ancients were the undisputed champions of waiting. If patience were an Olympic sport, they'd have gold medals forged from their own sweat and resigned sighs. These people didn't just wait—they *lived* waiting. It wasn't an inconvenience; it was just Thursday. Today, if Netflix buffers for three seconds, we turn into enraged philosophers of time and technology. "What is life if not an endless buffer circle?" But for our ancestors? Waiting was life's default setting, and whining about it was as effective as trying to train a cat to fetch.

Waiting for Food: Not DoorDash, Just Waiting

Today, if dinner doesn't appear within 30 minutes of clicking "Place Order," we morph into raging lunatics.. In Ancient Times, though, there was no such thing as "hurry up, I'm starving!" because, well, *everything* took forever. You didn't just wait for dinner to be served. You waited for the crops to grow, the weather to cooperate, the harvest to be gathered, and then–surprise–you spent hours grinding grain into flour, turning that flour into dough, and cooking it in a fire you probably spent the last two hours kindling. If you were hungry on Monday, you might eat on Thursday. If you were lucky.

Want meat? That required even more waiting: finding an animal, chasing it, spearing it, skinning it, and preparing it—all while simultaneously hoping you didn't become dinner for something bigger and faster. Let's not forget drying or smoking the meat for days to preserve it, because refrigeration? Please. That was called "winter."

Waiting for Communication: Not Instant Messaging, Just Hoping

If you think waiting for a text back is agonizing, let me introduce you to Ancient Rome. Imagine this: You send a letter—a scroll carefully penned by candlelight—to your friend two towns over. This letter is then entrusted to a sweaty, overworked messenger (probably named Gaius) who proceeds to jog for *days* to deliver your message.

You know when the reply comes? Maybe a month. Maybe never. Maybe Gaius gets eaten by wolves. Maybe your friend reads the letter, shrugs, and forgets to write back because she's busy grinding that grain we just talked about. And if you're waiting for important news—say, confirmation that your army isn't currently losing a war—you might as well make yourself comfortable because that reply is traversing entire empires on foot. You thought getting left on 'read' was bad? Try waiting six weeks just to get ghosted by someone in another empire.

Picture this conversation:

> **You**: "Has anyone heard from the front lines?"
>
> **Them**: "No."
>
> **You**: "When did we send a messenger?"
>
> **Them**: "Six weeks ago."
>
> **You**: "Cool. Should we panic?"
>
> **Them**: "Not yet. Give it a month."

To last, you had to wait. To be understood, you had to master the silence between moments. Patience was more than a virtue, it was the air people breathed.

In Athens, justice moved at the pace of molasses uphill. Trials weren't scheduled for a convenient time—you showed up and hoped for the best. If your name wasn't called, tough luck. Come back tomorrow. Even Socrates had to wait for his execution. They didn't just give him the poison—they had to wait for a special boat to return to Athens before they could legally kill him. Imagine being on death row, but your execution date depends on the ferry schedule.

When Waiting Meant a Three-Day Bender

Now, the ancients weren't all doom and gloom about waiting. In fact, they leaned into it, turning waiting into events—the original entertainment system.

Consider festivals, for example. You didn't just show up at noon for a two-hour party with finger foods. Nope, festivals were often multi-day affairs, sometimes even stretching weeks. It might be the spring solstice, so you're celebrating the planting season—and you *wait* for weeks for those first little sprouts to emerge from the soil. As history has proven, the best way to handle waiting is with fire and fermented liquids, you gather around fires, tell stories, drink questionable beverages, and dance your frustration away.

Or how about eclipses? Today, you get an app notification: "Partial eclipse in your area. Starts at 3:43 PM. Ends at 5:12 PM." Ancient people didn't have clocks or updates—just the sky and way too much time to overthink. Imagine them standing around, staring at the moon for hours like, "Any second now..." When something finally happened, they'd absolutely lose it: "The gods are furious!" "No, it's a blessing!" "Can someone just check if we're still planting the beans or what?"

Waiting wasn't just how life worked—it was their main hobby.

Transportation: Walking, Because That Was It

Modern waiting for transportation means sighing dramatically when Uber says, "6 minutes away." Ancient waiting? Oh, honey, they *were* the transportation.

Let's revisit poor Gaius, the Roman messenger. If he wanted to get somewhere, he walked. Horses were a luxury, and chariots were the ancient equivalent of a first-class flight—expensive and reserved for important people. For everyone else? You walked. Across valleys, mountains, deserts—sometimes with no sandals, no water bottles, and no playlist. Just you and your thoughts for *weeks*. And you know what? Gaius never rage-quit Rome with a one-star review: 'Too many hills, would not recommend.'

The ancient Egyptians had it even better (worse?) when they built the pyramids. Imagine the ultimate group project:

> **Pharaoh**: "So I need a giant pyramid. Tallest one yet. Should take 20 years."
>
> **Workers**: "Cool, and when do we get paid?"
>
> **Pharaoh**: "Oh, you get paid in grain. That you'll harvest yourselves. In about six months."

And they just accepted it. No one tried to unionize, and no one shouted, "We want our pyramid faster!"

Final Thoughts: Why They Waited Better Than Us

Here's the thing: The ancients didn't have a choice. Life was waiting. They couldn't speed up the sun, the crops, or a sweaty Gaius trekking across mountains with their messages. So they did what they could: they turned waiting into a craft. They made it ceremonial, communal, and—dare I say—spiritual.

Next time you find yourself losing your mind because it takes *15 minutes* for the waiter to bring bread to the table, remember this: You could've been waiting 15 *months* for bread to exist in the first place. And if the Netflix buffer circle taunts you, just close your eyes and think of Gaius, still running. Maybe light a candle for him. He probably deserves it.

In the next chapter we will head to medieval Europe where waiting wasn't merely a nuisance—it was practically a government policy. Tighten your corset and prepare for some historical nonsense. From feudal bureaucracy to endless pilgrimages, the Middle Ages perfected the art of making people wait. Want to travel? Better start walking now. Need an answer from your lord? Hope you enjoy suspense. Hungry? Well, let's just say fast food wasn't a thing unless you counted catching a rabbit with your bare hands. Welcome to a time when patience wasn't just a virtue—it was mandatory for survival.

Chapter Two

Medieval Waiting: Lords, Loaves, and Long Journeys

"Knights in white satin, never reaching the end."
– The Moody Blues, Nights in White Satin
(Medieval knights: the original long-haul commuters, except instead of traffic, they had bandits, dysentery, and the occasional fire-breathing dragon delaying their estimated arrival time to 'whenever the prophecy is fulfilled.')

If the ancients were the original waiters, medieval folk took waiting to a whole new level—adding layers of bureaucracy, feudal hierarchy, and religious obligations to ensure everyone was waiting *all the time*. Feudal life was essentially structured like a very long, confusing line: everyone waiting for someone else to make a decision, deliver news, or just acknowledge their existence.

Serfs: Waiting for the Lords (and the Lords' Decisions)

Life as a medieval serf was basically one big game of "Hurry Up and Wait." You spent your days waiting for your lord to tell you what to do, waiting for taxes to be collected, waiting for permission to get married, and—oh, yes—waiting for the smallest scraps of food to be handed back to you after toiling endlessly in the fields.

You: "May I marry Mildred?"

Lord: "I'll think about it."

You: "How long will that take?"

Lord: "How long is a harvest season?"

Decisions at the top trickled down at a pace that would make glaciers look zippy. Kings consulted their councils; councils consulted their bishops; bishops consulted their very complicated opinions on sin and taxation. By the time a decision was made, you probably forgot why you asked in the first place.

Waiting wasn't just a bureaucratic headache—it was law. Literally. Medieval justice worked on the principle of "we'll get to it when we get to it." If you were accused of a crime, you could spend months in a dungeon waiting for a trial that might never happen—because, well, the judge was busy with a jousting tournament, a crusade, or some other bullshit. Meanwhile, you sat there, contemplating life, hygiene, and whether mold counts as a food group.

Travel: Waiting on the Road (and Surviving the Journey)

Traveling in medieval times was a commitment that required an actual calendar and an ungodly amount of patience. If you wanted to visit a nearby town 20 miles away, you weren't planning a day trip; you were planning a *week*. Roads were terrible, bandits were plentiful, and your noble steed? Probably an underfed donkey who was in no hurry to get anywhere. The wheels of wagons broke, rivers flooded, and the weather did whatever it wanted without a shred of concern for your timeline.

Longer journeys, like pilgrimages, were epic undertakings—the medieval version of taking a long road trip to find yourself, but without the road, the car, or the luxury of stopping for gas station snacks. People spent months or *years* walking to far-off religious sites to pray for salvation or forgiveness.

> **Pilgrim**: "I'm walking to Canterbury to pray for my soul."
>
> **Friend**: "How long will that take?"
>
> **Pilgrim**: "What's time when eternity is at stake?"

In other words: don't wait up.

Waiting for Salvation: Religious Patience and Pilgrimages

Speaking of pilgrimages, waiting wasn't just practical—it was *spiritual*. Medieval people turned waiting into a path to enlightenment, a literal act of devotion. Walking thousands of miles to visit a relic of St. Somebody-or-Other wasn't seen as an inconvenience; it was symbolic. They waited in body as they did in spirit—for salvation, for miracles, or, at the very least, for a warm bed at the next abbey.

Medieval monks took waiting to an entirely different level. Ever heard of a silent retreat? Monasteries often required monks to spend years in quiet contemplation, patiently awaiting divine wisdom—or perhaps just hoping someone would invent chairs with cushions. After ten years of silence, Brother Alric was *this* close to unlocking the secrets of the universe. Then someone sneezed, and he had to start over.

Final Thoughts: Medieval Patience in Perspective

Today, if the WiFi drops out for five minutes, we consider throwing our router into the nearest river. In medieval times, rivers were just another thing you had to wait to cross. Life was slow, unpredictable, and at the mercy of nature, lords, and bishops. But instead of fighting it, medieval people embraced waiting as part of existence.

Patience wasn't a virtue—it was mandatory for survival. If you needed food, you waited for crops to grow. If you needed justice, you waited for the court to convene. If you needed salvation, well... you waited for divine intervention.

Next up, all aboard for the Industrial Revolution—the era that promised to make everything faster, smoother, and more efficient. Instead, it just gave us train schedules, factory whistles, and a whole new way to be late.

Chapter Three

Industrial Revolution: Waiting in an Age of Speed

"I hear the train a comin', it's rolling 'round the bend."
– Johnny Cash, *Folsom Prison Blues*
(Much like early industrial commuters, except instead of prison, they were trapped in a never-ending cycle of shift work, soot, and train delays.)

The medieval world was defined by slow, deliberate waiting, the Industrial Revolution came along, slammed a tankard of mead on the table, and shouted, "Faster, louder, more annoying!" Waiting didn't disappear—it just got noisier and a whole lot more complicated.

If medieval people were stuck waiting for their lords to make decisions, the Industrial Revolution arrived with a new message: "Good news! No more waiting for feudal bureaucracy! Bad news? Now, instead of waiting for the village blacksmith to finish your horseshoes at a leisurely pace, you were standing in line at a textile mill, watching the clock, and praying your 12-hour shift would end before your sanity did."

At least in the factory, you knew when your shift ended. A medieval serf asking for a day off? Well, let's just say Mildred's still waiting for an answer.

The Industrial Revolution was supposed to make everything faster. And it did. Trains screamed across landscapes at speeds that made cows faint (or so legend has it). Factories churned out goods with the relentless efficiency of an over-caffeinated hamster wheel. Suddenly, life moved faster—but with speed came an ironic twist: we found ourselves waiting *more*, just in entirely new ways.

All Aboard! Now Form a Line

Before the Industrial Revolution, there were fewer queues because, frankly, there were fewer places to go. You didn't queue for a horse ride to town—you just grabbed the horse and hoped it cooperated. But the railroads changed all that. Trains were punctual (well, *aspirationally* punctual), and suddenly humans had timetables to follow. People lined up to buy tickets, waited on crowded platforms, and stared down tracks with growing impatience, searching for the black dot of an approaching train like it was the world's first suspense thriller.

And yet, trains were magnificent! Before railroads, the average person never traveled faster than a goat at full trot. When locomotives hit 30 miles per hour, people feared their faces would melt off. Travelers would grip their hats, hold their breath, and brace for the unknown, screaming internally as they raced past fields of confused sheep while silently accepting that their souls might get left behind somewhere near mile marker five. Speed had arrived! So had the first "what the hell" moment of modern travel: how do you pass time waiting for something that moves faster than time itself... but still manages to be late?

"You want me to wait... *on purpose*?" passengers muttered as railway staff invented the queue. This, naturally, was just the warm-up act for the 21st-century airport line where you now wait for a TSA bag check to hand over an oversized bottle of shampoo, which no one *waited for* back in the day because no one *had* shampoo. Progress!

Factories: Where Time Became the Boss

Factory owners looked at people and said, "What if we took all the waiting out of *your* life and stuffed it into one big room?" And thus, the factory line was born. Goods came together faster than ever, but workers were introduced to a new kind of waiting—waiting for shifts to start, shifts to end, and for the clock to announce salvation in the form of a whistle-blow.

It was in the factory that waiting became regimented: *"Clock in at 7:00 AM sharp. Don't be late, or we'll deduct half a day's pay. Clock out at 7:00 PM. Also, don't be late, or we'll deduct half a day's pay.*" And just like that, the modern workplace began its centuries-long campaign to marry precision with punishment.

Clocking in itself became a spectacle. Early time clocks were strange contraptions: you slid a card in, the machine stamped the exact second of your arrival, and judgment was passed. If you were two minutes late, you were considered lazy; if you were thirty minutes early, you were suspicious. The time clock had no room for nuance, like, "I stopped to save a cat stuck in a well." Time didn't care. Time had trains to catch.

This rigid system turned waiting into something both dreaded and absurd. People would stand outside factory gates before dawn, shivering and staring at the looming hands of the clock, wondering why humans had invented time just to make it so oppressively important.

The Birth of the Commute: Why Are We All Here?

Before the Industrial Revolution, people lived where they worked. If you were a farmer, your commute was the seven steps it took to get from bed to field. But then factories happened. Cities ballooned with workers, and towns were built around railways, leading to a world-changing invention: the commute.

The idea of everyone being forced to travel at the exact same time was so revolutionary, it took people a few decades to realize how much it sucked. Imagine thousands crammed into carriages, inhaling the scent of each other's hastily eaten breakfasts, all while pondering the existential dread of synchronized labor.

Commuters learned to stare out windows stoically, perfecting that dreamy gaze that says, "I'm imagining a life where I'm not sitting next to someone whose breath smells like greasy spoiled eggs." Time slows down because your brain, deprived of stimulation, starts obsessing over the smallest (and occasionally smelliest) details.

Trains were so *reliable* that people began relying on them too much. Miss your train? Well, tough shit. Hope you enjoy unemployment. Entire days revolved around the rhythm of arrivals and departures, turning the train schedule into a sacred text. Some commuters even perfected the art of running *just in time* for the train doors to close in their faces. Waiting was now both a punishment for being too late and a reward for being *just a little too early*.

Clocking In—A Precursor to Modern Timekeeping

Meet Bob, your average factory worker in Manchester, circa 1842. Bob hated clocks. Before factory life, he could wake up, wander into his field, and yell at cows whenever he pleased. Now? He had to be at work precisely at 6:58 AM.

At 6:59, Bob stood in line with 20 other Bobs, each holding a card, waiting to *clock in*.
Ka-CHUNK. First Bob.
Ka-CHUNK. Second Bob.
By the third Bob, everyone was already annoyed—not at the wait, but at the ear-splitting sound of bureaucracy in action. By Bob #10, chaos broke out as they accused each other of "hogging the clock." Management intervened with a memo titled: "How to Wait in Line Like a Gentleman."

Bob's revenge? He started showing up late on purpose. And thus, the noble art of strategic lateness was born.

The factory time clock was modernity's way of whispering, "You are no longer the master of your time." The Industrial Revolution—the age of speed—made us faster workers, faster travelers... and somehow, even slower waiters. Waiting wasn't abolished; it was just industrialized.

The Irony of Speed

The Industrial Revolution accelerated goods, transportation, and life itself. Yet, with all this speed, it introduced the queue, the commute, and the factory clock—monuments to our knack for inventing new ways to stand around doing nothing. Fast forward to today: we've advanced so much, yet here we are—still waiting. For loading screens. For WiFi signals. For the driver ahead to look up from their damned phone and notice the light has turned green. Progress marches on, doesn't it?

Chapter Four

Fast Times to Buffering Wheels

Waiting from the mid 20th Century to Your Latest App Update

"I still haven't found what I'm looking for."
– U2, I Still Haven't Found What I'm Looking For
(Same, Bono. Still searching for the end of this stinkin' line, actually.)

For most of human history, waiting wasn't just an inconvenience—it was the default setting. Then, at some point in the late 20th century, we collectively decided that patience was for suckers and that every delay was a personal attack.

Look, I get it. No one likes waiting. But once upon a time, we had no choice, and somehow, we survived. Did it build character? Maybe. Did it make us stronger? Debatable. But at the very least, most of the time, we didn't completely unravel when we had to sit through a five-minute answering machine message just to hear "Hey, call me back."

The 20th century was really a transitional era for waiting—a time when patience was both a virtue and an inconvenience. People waited for world wars to end, for technology to improve, and for television antennas to stop turning them into human lightning rods. Waiting wasn't just a part of life—it *was* life. If you weren't waiting for something, you were probably dead.

Chicago Cubs fans understand this better than anyone. We waited 108 years to win a World Series. Entire generations lived and died without seeing it happen. Babies were born, grew up, had their own kids, retired, and still never saw a championship. When the Cubs finally won in 2016, I half-expected the universe to collapse in on itself just out of sheer confusion.

World War II: Waiting with a Purpose

Waiting back then was noble. Folks waited in ration lines for essentials—like sugar, butter, and a good excuse to complain about the neighbors cutting in line. You didn't get text alerts when food arrived. You just *hoped*.

Soldiers' families sent handwritten letters to the front lines, which traveled at the speed of a constipated tortoise looking for a bathroom. Months later, they'd finally get a reply: *"Dear Family, Still alive. Very muddy. Love, Joe."* That was it. And you cried tears of joy because at least Joe wasn't blown up!

Families waited for letters the way we now wait for Amazon packages—except instead of 'Out for

Delivery,' the update was more like 'Maybe still alive? TBD.' You think waiting for a pizza delivery is stressful? Try waiting for World War II to end.

Postwar Boom: Technology Taunts Us

After the war, they told us technology would make waiting obsolete. What a load of crap. Sure, we had new gadgets—but they mostly just gave us new things to wait for. Television signals. Road trips. The one working gas pump in a 50-mile radius. Progress? Maybe. Faster? Not exactly.

Televisions were huge wooden boxes that weighed as much as a small elephant. You had to fiddle with rabbit-ear antennas to get a signal, and God help you if someone walked by while you were watching. One misplaced step, and the signal vanished—turning your TV screen into static snow while you screamed 'DON'T MOVE!' like you were diffusing a bomb. Changing the channel meant you had to *get up*, turn a dial, and then sit back down—can you imagine? Then, only to realize you'd picked the wrong channel!

Cars took forever to save up for, and road trips were a test of endurance. Seat belts were optional, air conditioning was a roll-down window, and GPS didn't exist. We had paper maps—giant accordion-folded nightmares. If you got lost, you just yelled at Dad while he screamed back, "I know where I'm going!" He did not. And when the gas ran out, you didn't panic—you sat by the side of the road eating squished peanut butter sandwiches and waved at passing cars like you were hosting a picnic no one else was invited to.

Microwaves? Ha! Food took hours to cook, and ovens only had two settings: "cold" and "smelting furnace." You waited 45 minutes for a baked potato and then immediately burned your mouth because patience has limits.

Pop Culture: Waiting Takes Center Stage

The 20th century turned waiting into *art*. Samuel Beckett wrote a play called *Waiting for Godot*, where two guys wait around for someone who never shows up. Highbrow critics called it a profound meditation on the human condition. The rest of us just called it "a Tuesday."

Movies weren't much better. Alfred Hitchcock made waiting terrifying. He turned doorknobs, staircases, and ticking clocks into instruments of pure dread. As suspense built both on and off the screen, theatergoers waited for the big reveal… which usually amounted to someone screaming in black and white.

And literature? Forget it. Novels were 800-page marathons of people waiting for love, for death, or for the *plot* to happen. You'd get three chapters of someone staring wistfully at a field. If you were lucky, by chapter four, a sheep showed up.

Back then, we didn't have fancy smartphones or high-speed internet. Nope. Our phones were physically attached to the wall like some kind of landlocked sea creature. If you needed privacy, you'd stretch that tangled cord across the house, trip over the dog, knock over a lamp, and nearly took out a sibling in the process—only to have your mom pick up the other line anyway.

And GPS? Pfft. We had maps the size of bed sheets. You unfolded them once and never got them folded back. When you got lost, you didn't freak out—you embraced it. Getting lost was just how we discovered "scenic routes" and gas stations that sold boiled peanuts.

So yes, I remember most of this crap—well, what's left of my memory anyway. Waiting back then was inconvenient, inefficient, and *sometimes life-threatening*. All that waiting built patience and resilience—or so we thought. Then the 21st century arrived, laughed in our faces, and said: 'You want fast? Oh, I'll give you fast.'

The Age of Instant Gratification

Why does waiting feel worse today than it did 50 years ago? Let that question marinate for a second—or, in today's terms, about as long as it takes you to refresh your Instagram feed and discover that Jill from accounting has once again perfected her sourdough starter. Waiting, it seems, has become the modern-day equivalent of torture-by-paper-cut.

We live in a world of one-click purchases, same-day delivery, and high-speed everything. Instant coffee? Too slow. You're frothing milk like a barista while your smart coffee maker syncs up with your alarm clock. Need a ride? A stranger in a Toyota Corolla is already halfway to your house, probably regretting their life choices. Want to know the answer to the meaning of life? Google has it in 0.0032 seconds—The answer is 42, by the way. It's all right there—instant answers, instant coffee, instant rage when the WiFi lags for half a second. We have everything now, and somehow, waiting seems to sting more than ever before.

Let's be clear: our ancestors did not exactly live lives of luxury when it came to timelines. They waited months for letters that may or may not arrive, spent hours simmering beans on wood-burning stoves, and entertained themselves by staring at the wall and hoping their crops didn't die. And if you wanted a product that wasn't in stock? Tough. You just waited—like a saint, a monk, or someone without social media.

But here's the thing: waiting times today aren't necessarily longer than they were in the past. In fact, in many cases, they're shorter. What *has* changed are our expectations. Once you've experienced the dopamine hit of instant gratification, the bar for patience drops lower than a limbo stick at a beach party.

Think about it. Fifty years ago, if you wanted a book, you went to the library. If it was checked out, you waited. Days passed, perhaps weeks. You adapted. Now? If your Amazon package isn't on your doorstep within 12 hours, you start acting like you've been personally betrayed by Jeff Bezos.

So why does waiting seem worse today? Because we've conditioned ourselves to expect *everything* faster, cheaper, and on-demand. Our brains have rewired to think, "Why wait when you don't have to?" It's not just about convenience; it's about our perceived control—our status as self-proclaimed masters of time. Waiting is no longer a pause; it's an interruption—an affront to our efficiency, amplified by our obsession with *scroll culture* and the endless churn of *hyper-posting hubs* that keep us perpetually refreshing, swiping, and waiting for the next dopamine hit. And, as a species, we're now allergic to being interrupted.

From Cavemen to Karens: The Downfall of Our Patience

Picture this: a caveman (aka an early human who happens to live in a cave) waiting for fire. He's sitting there rubbing sticks together, sweating like he just ran a marathon in a leopard-skin onesie. Days pass.

He's hungry, cold, and probably being heckled by saber-toothed squirrels. But does he scream, *"WHERE'S MY FIRE?!"* and angrily refresh his sticks? No. He waits. Because fire takes time.

Now imagine that same caveman—except he's in line at Starbucks today. His name gets skipped, and suddenly, he's pacing like a caged animal. His breath is shallow. His fists clench. *"FIVE MINUTES?!"* He mutters darkly. *"They're doing this on purpose!"* The barista *clearly* has a vendetta against him. He checks his watch. He doesn't wear a watch. His primal instincts kick in. He contemplates storming the counter and demanding justice, or he'll start a Yelp war. He is unraveling. And so are we.

This is us. We are that caveman, minus the sticks, plus an unhealthy addiction to oat milk lattes.

The Emotional Devastation of Waiting 45 Extra Seconds for a Burrito

But how did we go from creatures who patiently grew crops for food to absolute maniacs who yell at Alexa for taking too long to set a timer? Let me tell you: somewhere between dial-up internet and same-day shipping, we all lost our fucking collective marbles.

It's not just technology's fault, either—though tech certainly *lit the fuse*. The people who brought us instant streaming, overnight delivery, and *Tinder* (the dating app where you judge people's entire life potential in 0.2 seconds) looked at patience and said:

"Fuck it. It's dead to us. Burn it to the ground."

And we, like well trained golden retrievers started wagging our tails and clapping our hands. "Faster? Yes, please! Hook that dopamine straight into my veins!"

Now here's where it gets bonkers: the more instant gratification we get, the angrier we become when anything takes longer than expected. Patience used to be a virtue; now it's an *endangered species*. If there's a buffering symbol on Netflix, we become full-blown philosophers, questioning time, space, and our place in the universe staring at the screen whispering, *"Why do bad things happen to good people?"*

And can we talk about microwaves again? They are already miraculous. You put in cold, soggy leftovers, press a button, and BAM—nuclear heat in 90 seconds. Do we marvel at this modern wizardry? No. We stand there, arms crossed, glaring at the countdown like it's a hostage negotiation. We don't even let it finish!

Five, four, three—BEEP! Nope! Door open. I'll decide when my burrito is ready, thank you.

Congratulations, We've Lost Our Damn Minds

It's gotten so bad that our expectations have outpaced reality. You ever track a package and get mad when it says "Out for Delivery" but *still* isn't at your doorstep? It's on a truck, for crying out loud, crawling through traffic—but somehow, in your mind, that driver is *deliberately avoiding you.* I swear, if we could call and FaceTime the UPS guy, we would. *"Hi, Kevin. I was the next stop twenty minutes ago. What the fuck? Where are you? I just want to talk."*

Ironically, all our efforts to eliminate waiting just made it more maddening. Now we obsess over it. When you order food, the app shows you a tiny little map of your driver's progress. It's like watching Santa Claus, except instead of gifts, you're tracking a burrito bowl. "Why did they turn left? They turned LEFT? That wasn't on the route—Are they lost?!" "Are they joyriding with my burrito bowl?" Should I call them? No, that's crazy. (...Or is it?) By the time they arrive, you're shaking, drenched in sweat, and you practically tackle the driver with gratitude.

This is not normal.

Here's the truth no one wants to hear: impatience is the ultimate self-sabotage. When you expect the entire world to sprint, you miss the joy of the jog. It's like being at Disneyland and complaining about the wait for Space Mountain, forgetting that the wait *is the experience*. You're in line with friends, eating a churro for God's sake, eavesdropping on the family next to you. The waiting is where the stories happen.

But impatience? Impatience turns us into lunatics. It's why we honk the millisecond a red light turns green, or scream at a webpage that's taking longer to load than it takes for a sloth to finish its breakfast. Impatience ruins the moments that are already in front of us—because instead of living them, we're too busy foaming at the mouth, tapping our watches like they'll bend time itself.

Deep breaths Rick, OK I'm back... So what if waiting isn't the enemy? What if it's actually the antidote—the universe's way of throwing us a mandatory timeout so we can take a breath, think a thought, and, I don't know... be human for five seconds?

We'll get into that. But first, put your damn phone down. Staring at your UPS tracker won't make your burrito bowl materialize faster. Let's embrace the pause together.

Because here's the thing—waiting isn't the villain we've made it out to be. Impatience is. It's why your blood pressure spikes when the pizza delivery tracker doesn't update fast enough. But what if, instead of waging war on waiting, we learned to use it?

In the next section, we're going to dig into the surprising ways waiting—yes, waiting—can be a gift. I know, I know, right? A gift? Like socks at Christmas? Trust me. By the end, you might find yourself actually *looking forward* to those moments of pause. Or, at the very least, you'll yell at the microwave a little less. Baby steps.

Now, let's move on—but, you know, not too fast.

Waiting as a Gift—Yes, Seriously

Alright, stay with me here. I know you're skeptical. Calling waiting a *gift* might sound like calling a paper cut a "learning opportunity" or describing traffic jams as "group meditation." You're not buying it. I get it. But what if I told you that waiting is basically the universe's most underappreciated gift bag? You're not *stuck*. You're being handed a pocket of time. A secret little slice of life where nothing else is expected of you except *to be*. Like an all-expenses-paid mindfulness retreat that you didn't ask for and probably didn't want, but hey—it's free.

Here's the thing: we're terrible at waiting because we've been trained to think that life is a productivity contest. Every minute needs to be milked for its full potential. Hustle culture whispers things like, "What do you mean you're waiting for a train? Start a side hustle on that train platform! Write your memoir on the back of a receipt while you wait!" It's exhausting.

We've convinced ourselves that waiting is wasted time, when really, it's bonus time. Like finding a $5 bill in the laundry. Unexpected, unplanned, but still delightful.

The Lost Art of Doing Absolutely Nothing

Imagine this: you're stuck in line at the DMV. Classic nightmare scenario. The guy in front of you is sighing dramatically like he's auditioning for a one-man play called *Why Me?* Behind you, someone is loudly FaceTiming a relative who seems to be shouting back. You're trapped in the middle, a reluctant member of this DMV improv troupe. And yet—this moment is actually a gift.

Let me explain. You're in line. You're not *driving*. You're not *answering emails*. You're not *folding laundry* or *being productive* in any traditional sense. You are simply *there*. Your job is to exist and advance one slow shuffle at a time. This is an incredibly rare phenomenon. Life has presented you with a moment where you can't do much *except* notice things. The musty, well-worn carpet that looks like it was last vacuumed when the original Star Wars trilogy was still in theaters. The scuffed linoleum that is so worn down, if you listen closely, you can hear it sigh in resignation every time someone takes a step on it. The quiet comedy of watching someone try to make small talk with a

DMV employee—a Sisyphean task if ever there was one.

It's like this weird cosmic pause button. And instead of raging against it, you can choose to lean in. Observe the absurdity. Smile at it. Take a breath. DMV time is still your time—just without the pressure to do *anything useful* with it. A no-cost invitation to witness the slow-motion divine comedy of existence.

Obviously, this doesn't just happen in the DMV. Waiting sneaks up on us everywhere. The doctor's office. Airports. Coffee shop lines. The grocery store when the person ahead of you decides *now* is the perfect time to test out a thousand coupons and argue about cantaloupe pricing. Instead of fuming, what if you reframed it? What if you thought, "Oh good—a moment to pause." And yes, I know—"pausing" sounds suspiciously like something a wellness influencer would market as 'sacred stillness' in a $400 jar. But bear with me.

Pausing doesn't mean being a Zen master. It means noticing. It means hearing the absurd elevator music playing in a waiting room and thinking, '*Wow, someone actually composed this shit... on purpose.*' It means seeing the guy ahead of you in shorts wearing black socks with sandals and admiring his sheer confidence. It means staring at the shelf of candy bars next to the checkout line and wondering, *Why does no one ever buy a Milky*

Way? How did Milky Way lose its mojo? I used to love Milky Way, I'm gonna buy one.

In these little moments, you're alive to the world in a way you might otherwise miss. You're not rushing past it. You're *in it*. Waiting makes you present. And let's be honest—you could use some presence. We all could. Have you *seen* how much time we spend staring at our phones, trying to pretend we're not waiting? If aliens landed tomorrow, they'd assume the human species was born surgically attached to a rectangle and powered entirely by thumbs. Perhaps we need to put the rectangle down and just... exist.

You might even start to enjoy it. The pause. The moment between moments. Waiting can be the breath you didn't know you needed. Like the calm before the storm of a busy day, or the stillness after someone finally stops snoring. It's a gift because it's a reminder: not every second has to be accounted for. Not every minute has to be optimized. Life isn't a checklist. It's the moments in between—the absurd, slow, silly ones that remind us we're alive.

Instead of huffing, puffing, or Googling the weather for cities you don't live in, try this: take a deep breath, look around, and think, *This is it. A tiny, silly slice of life. A moment to just be.* Waiting might not be the gift you wanted—but it's the gift you've got.

And who knows? Embrace it, you might unwrap something unexpected along the way. And if not...

well, at least unwrap the damn Milky Way you've been obsessing about.

Because here's the truth: waiting isn't simply the space between moments—it *is* the moment. It's life happening in real time. And if we stopped treating it like an obstacle, maybe, we'd stop racing past the best parts before we even realize they're gone.

In the next chapter, we'll take a world tour of countries where waiting is practically an art form. From leisurely queues to tea-sipping pauses, you'll discover strategies that might just make you *savor* the wait... or at least fake it like a pro.

Part II

The Cultural, Philosophical, and Emotional Dimensions of Waiting

Chapter Five
Around the World in 80 Queues

"Turn off your mind, relax, and float downstream."
- The Beatles, *Tomorrow Never Knows*
(*Exactly what Japanese commuters do silently standing perfectly aligned waiting for a train*)

If there's one thing the world agrees on, it's that waiting is a universal experience—like endless lines at the DMV, the buffering wheel showing up right as the game-winning play unfolds, and hitting every red light when you're already five minutes late. Yet, while some countries approach waiting with clenched teeth and silent suffering (*ahem*, America), other nations have turned waiting into fine art. It's as if they collectively said, "Why waste good frustration when we can channel it into something weirdly enjoyable?"

Waiting is the one thing that unites humanity across borders. From Japan's silent subway queues to Greece's expressive café rants, every culture has its own way of dealing with life's unskippable pauses. Some embrace the wait; others fight it like it owes them money. So, let's take a trip around the world to explore how certain enlightened countries have hacked the eternal pause button—no passport required, just patience.

Sweden: Lagom Means Never Losing Your Cool

Ah, Sweden: the land of IKEA and ABBA, and a mysterious knack for handling life's little delays with the patience of a monk assembling a 400-piece bookshelf. If you've ever wondered why Swedes can wait for hours without so much as a twitch, the answer lies in their cultural superpower—Lagom. It's like a built-in chill mode, but with fewer deep breaths and more cinnamon buns.

Lagom, the untranslatable word that means "just the right amount," is the Swedish philosophy of life. Not too much, not too little—just enough to make waiting bearable, even enjoyable. Pair it with fika, the sacred coffee-and-pastry ritual, and you'll start to see why Swedes are the Olympic gold medalists of waiting.

The Waiting Game, Swedish Style

Picture it. You've taken a number and realized there are 47 people ahead of you. In most countries, this would cause groans, sighs, or compulsive Instagram scrolling. In Sweden, it's a Lagom moment—a chance to ponder life's deeper questions, like how many streaming subscriptions are *the perfect right amount* before you've officially gone too far. You'll spend the time marveling at how even this wait feels perfectly tuned to your inner philosopher.

The IKEA meatball line is the ultimate Lagom testing ground. Too fast, and you'd miss the chance to contemplate how many Billy bookcases one person truly needs. Too slow, and you'd risk hanger. But in Sweden, the line moves at a Lagom pace—just brisk enough to leave you peacefully content and, probably, mentally drafting a heartfelt ode to lingonberry jam.

Lagom: The Jedi Mind Trick for Life's Annoyances

A train delay in Sweden is not a reason for panic but a divine invitation for fika. It's a great time to grab yourself a coffee and a cinnamon bun, and enjoy the wait. In Sweden, you don't kill time, you party with it. Where else can you say, "The train's late? Sweet! More fika!" and actually be thrilled? Swedes don't fight waiting—they simply out-chill it.

Swedes don't overwork—they Lagom work. Staying late to impress your boss? Amateur move. In Sweden, this behavior triggers concern. "Are you okay? Is everything fine at home?" Overworking is a red flag that you haven't mastered the art of balance. Productivity in Sweden is about getting the right amount done—anything more or less is considered suspiciously un-Lagom.

Swedes excel at Lagom mingling. Conversations are polite, engaging, and never monopolized.

Over-enthusiasm is as frowned upon as awkward silences.

Swedes Lagom their way to saving the planet. Smaller homes, second-hand goods, and biking to work aren't trends—they're lifestyles.

Lagom turns waiting into a sport—why stress when you can sip coffee, reflect on life, or just stare into space like a pro? Swedes don't battle delays; they hug them like an old friend, turning every pause into a perfectly brewed moment of zen. Why rush? The best bits of life are the ones in between. And if all else fails, fika saves the day—with coffee and a cinnamon bun, everything's Lagom again.

While Sweden has mastered the art of balanced patience, Jamaica takes a different approach—one that involves fewer deep sighs and more reggae. If Sweden's waiting style is a perfectly arranged bookshelf, Jamaica's is a hammock swaying in the breeze. Let's loosen up and head south, where waiting isn't merely accepted—it's straight-up enjoyed.

Jamaica: Turning Waiting into an Irie State of Mind

Jamaica: the land of reggae, jerk chicken, and a vibe so laid-back it makes a hammock look stressed. If you've ever wondered how Jamaicans handle waiting without losing their cool, the secret is simple—they turn every delay into an opportunity to bask in life's chill moments. Because here, everything is irie, mon.

And what is irie, you ask? It's more than just a word; it's a whole mood. Irie means everything is good, life is sweet, and the vibes are flowing like rum punch at a beach party. It's not only about being okay—it's about being so okay that even waiting in line seems like a mini vacation.

Irie In Action

You've been waiting an hour past your appointment time, but no one's breaking a sweat—not even you. Why? Because this is Jamaica, where "soon come" is a way of life. Grab a patty from the vendor outside, chat up a fellow patient, or simply enjoy the reggae station playing softly in the corner. Time isn't running out—it's just stretching its legs.

The line for jerk chicken is long, but who's in a hurry? The smoky aroma teases your senses, guaranteeing it'll be worth every second. You trade jokes with the the guy next to you in line and groove a little to the reggae beats in the background. Why stress when the wait is already marinated in good vibes?

Even the beach has its queues—like waiting for your turn at the jerk stand or for someone to finally return the snorkel gear. But in Jamaica, this is no big deal. You're on island time, sipping a cold Red Stripe and letting the slow rhythm of the waves remind you that life is already perfect.

Jamaicans have mastered the balance between effort and ease. The motto? Work hard, but don't let it cramp your vibe. Deadlines will come and go, but so will another round of rum punch at the after-work hangout. "Relax, mon. The deadline's tomorrow. Let it breathe."

Jamaicans don't simply wait—they vibe through it. Every delay is an excuse to slow down, enjoy the moment, and connect with those around you. Whether it's a missed bus, a long line, or a delayed flight, the Jamaican spirit transforms it into a chance to soak up life.

In Jamaica, time takes orders from you, not the other way around. Add some good company, great food, and reggae floating through the air, and suddenly, life feels exactly as it should.

If Jamaica turns waiting into a laid-back groove, Denmark turns it into a Pinterest-worthy mood board. Where Jamaicans ride out delays with reggae and rum punch, Danes handle them with blankets, candles, and a borderline spiritual devotion to coziness. Let's leave the sunshine behind and head north—where waiting isn't only tolerated, it's *hygge-fied*.

Denmark: Hygge Your Wait Away

In Denmark, they take cozy vibes so seriously that they invented *hygge* (pronounced somewhere between "hooga" and a satisfied sigh). If you think waiting is boring, the Danes would like you to reconsider. They would also like you to light a candle.

Waiting for a delayed train? Time to whip out a thermos of cocoa, snuggle into a wool blanket, and meditate on the beauty of raindrops sliding down the windowpane. After all, if you're going to wait, why not do it in style?

Waiting Rooms So Nice, You Forget Why You're There

You should check out the waiting rooms in Denmark. Unlike the harshly lit, stiff-chaired boredom chambers the rest of us endure, Danish waiting rooms look like they were curated by a Nordic design guru who believes even bureaucracy deserves mood lighting. The chairs are so comfortable, you briefly wonder if you've accidentally wandered into a high-end spa instead of a government office. The lamps emit a warm, golden glow that suggests everything will be okay.

Many waiting rooms have actual, crackling, cozy fireplaces. You walk in expecting a row of cold metal chairs and instead find yourself in what can only be described as a Scandinavian ski lodge that also happens to renew driver's licenses. Suddenly, you're sipping complimentary gourmet coffee, watching the flames flicker, and questioning whether you should take up journaling.

By the time your number is called, you're almost disappointed. You don't want to go back to the real world. You were prepared for a miserable errand, but Denmark handed you an impromptu self-care retreat. Honestly, if they threw in a foot massage, you'd start making up reasons to come back. But while the Danes have turned waiting into a spa day, Costa Rica takes a different approach. Over there, waiting isn't about candles and coziness—it's about leaning back, letting life unfold, and fully embracing the art of doing absolutely nothing.

Costa Rica: Cooler than a Cucumber in a Bowl of Ranch

Welcome to Costa Rica: the land of lush rainforests, stunning beaches, and a national vibe so chill it makes sloths look rushed. Here, the secret to happiness isn't about avoiding waiting—it's about embracing it. How? With pura vida, of course.

Pura vida translates to "pure life," but let's be real—it's more than that. It's Costa Rica's unofficial motto, state of mind, and possibly the greatest excuse for being late ever invented.

Delayed bus? *Pura vida*. Slow service? *Pura vida*. Left your keys inside while locking yourself out? Eh... sure if you say so, *pura vida*.

Pura vida is the ultimate stress deflector, keeping anxiety levels lower than a sunbathing iguana that's too lazy to move even when a coconut drops next to it. It's the national reminder that life is better when you don't fight time—or at the very least, when you don't let time boss you around like an overcaffeinated life coach.

Waiting, Costa Rican Style

The guide is running late, but no one's worried. Instead, you're soaking up the scenery, listening to the chirping of birds, and chatting with fellow adventurers about which waterfall hike is the best. Someone says, "Relax, pura vida," and you smile—because in Costa Rica, it's not about when the tour starts, but how much you enjoy the wait.

The kitchen is taking its time, but it doesn't matter. You're sipping fresh-squeezed guava juice, enjoying the ocean breeze, and wondering if life can possibly get better. It can—once that plate of gallo pinto arrives. Pura and simple, less is more.

Pura Vida: Where the National Speed Limit is 'Whenever'

Costa Ricans know how to balance work and play. Sure, they get the job done—but they don't let it get in the way of enjoying life. Stress? Never heard of it. Lunch breaks? Those are sacred. Picture a group of coworkers under a shady palm tree, laughing over fresh ceviche while arguing about whose uncle makes the best guaro. Work can wait—this is the real productivity.

Traffic in Costa Rica can be… let's call it "adventurous." But instead of honking or glaring, people roll down their windows, wave, and throw out a casual "Pura vida!" A three-car pile-up isn't a tragedy; it's a chance to bond with strangers while waiting for the road to clear.

A party doesn't start until everyone's truly ready—so showing up "on time" is optional. You're greeted with warm smiles, fresh fruit drinks, and a relaxed vibe that makes every gathering seem like a celebration of life itself.

In Costa Rica, you don't fight time—you slow dance with it. With the sun shining, good company nearby, and a fresh coconut never too far away, life simply unfolds at its own unhurried pace. Pura vida isn't something you schedule—it's something you sink into, whether you meant to or not.

While Costa Rica turns waiting into an extended happy hour, Finland treats it like a ritual in spiritual stillness—wrapped in snow, gently steamed in a sauna, and infused with the crisp scent of pine. The quiet is so deep, you might start hearing your own thoughts in surround sound. So trade your coconut drink for a deep breath of Arctic fresh air—we're heading from beachside relaxation to the kind of silence that feels freshly scrubbed, slightly forest-scented, and best accompanied by Van Morrison's *Hymns to the Silence*.

Finland: From Silent Bus Stops to Naked Sauna Bliss

While their Nordic neighbors hygge and lagom their way through waiting, the Finns prefer to wait in absolute, deafening silence. In Finland, silence is not awkward—it's a mark of respect. And nowhere is this clearer than when waiting.

Picture this: a Finnish bus stop in January. It's -25°C. There are four people standing six feet apart, motionless, staring into the void as if waiting for an existential revelation rather than public transportation. Nobody speaks. Nobody makes eye contact. It's the most respectful standoff you've ever seen.

And yet, right when you think the Finns might spontaneously combust from all that stoic restraint, they collectively head to the sauna. Yes, the very same people who avoided eye contact at the bus stop will now sit shoulder to shoulder—naked—in a steaming wooden room as if it's the most natural thing in the world. And it *is*. Finnish rule of thumb: avoid eye contact in public, then strip down and sweat with strangers. The logic? Don't question it—it's just Finland.

Sauna is where the Finnish magic happens. Time slows down. You sweat out your stress. Nobody feels the need to make awkward small talk because silence...is still golden. Combined with pristine nature, low crime rates, and an unwavering belief that less is more, Finland consistently tops the list of the world's happiest countries. Who knew silent waiting and steamy bonding could make for such a contented life?

Chill Hard, Live Long

Finland isn't simply cold—it's cool in every possible sense. While the rest of the world treats happiness like a frantic scavenger hunt, Finland plays it like a slow-burning, minimalist jazz album. The country has somehow cracked the code to joy, and the secret isn't wealth or sunshine (because, let's be honest, winter here lasts approximately 14 months). It's chill. Literal and metaphorical.

Finns don't rush. They don't overcomplicate things. They take their time, whether it's sipping a beer in a lakeside cabin, or spending half a day quietly existing in the woods. They embrace a philosophy of *kalsarikännit*, which roughly translates to "getting drunk at home alone in your underwear." Imagine a country where this is not a personal low point, but an endorsed lifestyle choice.

They also embrace *sisu*—a word that doesn't translate exactly but basically means "push through the hard stuff without whining." Life is cold? Layer up. Car buried under snow? Dig it out, one stoic shovel-full at a time.

The Secret to Happiness: Lower the Bar, Raise the Sauna Temperature

So why is Finland always ranked the happiest country in the world? Because the Finns don't define happiness as constant excitement or relentless positivity. Instead, it's about contentment, simplicity, and knowing when to shut the fuck up and sit in a hot wooden box.

Other countries chase happiness like it's an Olympic sport—Finns treat it like a well-stewed cup of tea. Maybe that's why, while everyone else is yelling at customer service or rage-refreshing a delivery tracker, Finland is just out there... existing. Patiently. Quietly. Probably in the snow.

We could all learn a thing or two from them.

Maybe patience in Finland is best summed up as "less is more"—less talking, less stress, less unnecessary movement, and somehow, more happiness. While the rest of the world is buzzing with urgency, Finns have mastered the art of simply *being*—whether it's in a silent forest, a dimly lit sauna, or standing in line with the kind of stillness that could convince you they're part of the landscape.

And then there's England, where waiting isn't about silence—it's about structure, order, and, most importantly, the queue.

England: Mastering the Queue with a Stiff Upper Lip and a Sense of Humor

Ah, England: the land of tea, crumpets, and the art of queuing perfected to Olympic standards. For the English, waiting isn't a nuisance—it's a tradition, a quiet sport where patience meets politeness. Rain pouring down while you queue for a bus? No problem, there's an umbrella for that. Train delayed? Time to grumble politely and have another biscuit.

Waiting, English Style

The queue is long, but no one's complaining—at least not out loud. Instead, you stand quietly, mentally ranking which biscuit reigns supreme (digestives vs. hobnobs, anyone?) while eyeing the person ahead of you, silently judging their choice of snacks, outfit, or how they're holding up the line. (By the way the answer is duh—hobnobs, obviously.)

Queuing is not only a cultural tradition in England—it's a moral imperative.

Here's how it works: A queue is sacred. It is orderly. It is just. And woe to the person who disrupts it. Step out of line or cut ahead, and you will not face physical violence; no, you will endure the far worse punishment of collective passive-aggressive huffing.

The English will not confront you directly. They will simply mutter phrases like, "Some people..." and "Well, that's bold," while pointedly refusing to look at you. Their judgment is silent, but it burns to your soul. By the time you reach the front, you'll wish you'd just stayed home.

English drivers handle traffic jams with the grace of a Jane Austen character at a ball. There's a bit of muttering, a tap on the steering wheel, but no one's honking. If it's really bad, they might roll their eyes and say something outrageous like, "Oh, for heaven's sake!"

The pub queue is where British politeness truly shines. No cutting, no shoving—just a polite "Who's next?" when the bartender glances up. Waiting for your pint is all part of the charm, and let's face it, the beer tastes better when you've earned it with impeccable queuing manners.

Tea Time: A Most Civilized Madness

No discussion of waiting in England would be complete without paying our respects to the greatest waiting ritual of them all: tea time. This isn't merely a break—it's a sacred rite, a national institution, a time-honored contract between civilization and sanity.

Meetings? Postponed.
Crises? Put on hold.
The fate of the universe? Let's not be too hasty.

Because when the kettle whistles, everything stops. If King Charles himself were escaping a burning building and someone offered him a cuppa, he'd take a moment to say, "Oh, go on then." Possibly followed by a heated debate about whether one should pour the milk first or last.

The Art of the Steep

Tea time isn't about endurance; it's about devotion. You don't just drink tea—you embark on a deliberate, multi-step ceremony in which every action is a test of your commitment to the cause.

1. Boil the water. (An impatient soul will start steeping before the rolling boil, and to them, I say: May the ancestors forgive you.)
2. Steep the tea. (For how long? The correct answer: Until it reaches the exact moment of peak flavor that you personally believe in, based on centuries of British intuition.)
3. Let it cool. (Ha! Just kidding. You will absolutely scald your tongue because patience is a virtue right up until you're thirsty.)
4. Milk or no milk? (This is where friendships are made and lost.)

And of course, the biscuits. Essential tools for pacing oneself, lest you commit the ultimate crime: finishing your tea before your hobnob has reached peak dunkability.

Because nothing is more truly, painfully British than miscalculating the structural integrity of a biscuit mid-dunk and watching in silent horror as it collapses into the cup—a soggy, irretrievable tragedy.

SIDE NOTE: The English have put centuries of thought into their biscuit of choice, but on the other side of the pond we have our own coffee dunking obsessions. A proper biscotti, a sturdy stroopwafel (which perches, not plunges), or, if you're really playing in the big leagues, Trader Joe's Oatmeal Cranberry Dunkers purpose-built for coffee immersion, with just the right amount of chew to hold up to the job. Don't forget the mighty Biscoff, the unsung hero of coffee dunking. That deep caramelized flavor, the crisp-but-not-too-crisp texture—this cookie was practically engineered to meet its fate in a steaming cup of coffee.

Have I put way too much thought into this? Probably. But if you've ever fished a half-dissolved cookie out of your coffee like a sunken treasure, you understand why this is serious business.

Waiting, Elevated to an Art Form

If the English have mastered the queue, then tea time is the Olympic final. The gold medal round of patience. A moment of national unity where we all pause, take a breath, and agree that, no matter how mad the world is, it must wait until we've finished our brew.

Because let's be honest: the best things in life—like a proper cup of tea, revenge, and a well-executed sarcastic remark—take time.

Always Look On The Bright Side of Life

Picture a group of strangers on a train platform, staring at the departure board with the dead-eyed resignation of people who have been here before. They know the drill. The train is delayed, again.

Someone sighs. Someone checks their watch. And then, like clockwork, the real British pastime begins: making jokes about it.

In England, waiting isn't simply endured—it's softened with humor. A quick quip about how train delays are part of an annual tradition gets the ball rolling. Someone adds, "Looks like summer's been canceled again!" and, without missing a beat, another chimes in, "Better than last year's six-hour heatwave!" Suddenly, the waiting feels less like a chore and more like open mic night at the comedy club.

As Eric Idle so wisely sang in *Monty Python's Life of Brian*, "Always look on the bright side of life." For the English, this isn't just a lyric—it's a way of life. Keep calm, carry on, and muddle your way through the wait!

Japan: Waiting as a Performance Art

Japan elevates waiting to an art form. Whether it's queuing for ramen or bullet trains, the Japanese have perfected the choreography of patience.

People line up in neat rows for Tokyo's trains, silently waiting for the doors to open. Once inside, they pack together like sardines but somehow remain perfectly composed, as if waiting itself were a chance to practice mindfulness.

This cultural reverence for order and patience stems in part from Zen Buddhism, which values presence and mindfulness. Waiting is part of the natural rhythm of life. In Japan, waiting isn't a burden—it's mastered. Whether it's a ramen line or a bullet train platform, every wait is proof that patience isn't only a virtue—it's a skill.

Four Hours, One Cup of Tea, and the Meaning of Life

If you think standing in a perfectly silent, impeccably organized train queue is peak Japanese patience, just wait until you hear about the tea ceremony—an event so precise, so structured, that even German engineers would break a sweat trying to keep up.

A Japanese tea ceremony isn't simply about making tea. It's an experience, a ritual, a spiritual event, and possibly the world's most polite endurance test. Every single movement—from how the tea is scooped, to how the bowl is turned before drinking—is choreographed with the precision of a NASA launch sequence. And don't even think about rushing it—each step is meant to be slow, deliberate, and deeply meaningful. It's basically the opposite of how the rest of us consume caffeine (*chugging coffee in a travel mug while running for the train like a deranged gazelle*).

Guests are expected to sit in serene contemplation, appreciating the delicate beauty of the moment, the tea, and possibly their own slowly numbing legs because traditional tea rooms require kneeling for *a very long time*. Meanwhile, the host moves with the grace of a samurai warrior who trained exclusively in the art of pouring liquid. And the best part? This whole process can take up to four hours.

Four. Hours. For one cup of tea.

And yet, no one complains. In Japan, waiting is elevated to a near-spiritual experience. The tea will be ready when it's ready, and if you're truly present, you'll realize that the waiting is just as important as the drinking. (*Or, at the very least, you'll achieve inner peace by accepting that you can no longer feel your feet.*)

Even better? Waiting in Japan is often rewarded. That ramen shop you waited two hours for? Life-changing. That bullet train you waited six minutes for? You're already in Kyoto. Japan proves that sometimes the wait is as beautiful as the thing you're waiting for—especially if it involves noodles.

In Japan, waiting is curated, refined, and executed with the precision of a perfectly raked Zen garden. Every delay is like one of those meticulously arranged sand patterns—calm, intentional, and absolutely not to be disturbed. Try to rush it, and you're basically the guy who trips and faceplants into the gravel. Waiting here isn't wasted time; it's just time...with better aesthetics.

Next up we head to Bhutan, where it's less about order and more about embracing the cosmic joke of time itself—because when your country measures success in Gross National Happiness instead of GDP, every delay is just the universe reminding you to chill.

Bhutan: The Happiest Wait in the World

Bhutan, the tiny Himalayan kingdom famous for prioritizing Gross National Happiness, has a refreshing take on waiting: if you're happy in the moment, what's the rush?

Here, delays are viewed through a philosophical lens. The Buddhist teachings that permeate Bhutanese culture emphasize mindfulness and the impermanence of all things—including delays. Imagine waiting for a government service surrounded by prayer wheels and chanting monks. Even the most mundane waits can come with a unique twist.

Traffic jams for instance, might involve an actual cow lounging in the middle of the road, unbothered by the growing traffic jam they've instigated. In true Bhutanese fashion, the people just simply wait for the cow to move in it's own leisurly pace and everyone has a good laugh of the absurdity of the situation. In Bhutan, you don't honk at the cow. You accept that this is life now—and honestly, life's pretty great. Bhutan's approach reminds us that waiting is a natural part of life, not an inconvenience.

It's hard to argue when you're surrounded by mountains, monks, and a cultural ethos that whispers, "Chill, friend even the yetis aren't in a hurry. Life is good."

Spain: Mañana Means Never Waiting Too Hard

In Spain, the concept of *mañana* ("tomorrow") reigns supreme. If something doesn't happen today... well, there's always tomorrow. Waiting is less about patience and more about accepting that clocks are merely suggestions.

Waiting for a friend to show up? Relax. They'll be there when they're there. Waiting for dinner? It'll happen at 10 p.m., but hey, tapas are a fine way to kill time. And then, of course, there's the *siesta*—the glorious national tradition of taking a nap in the middle of the day. Why wait for something when you can just... sleep through it? In Spain, clocks are only suggestions. If you show up 'on time,' you're the weird one. Why rush, when there's wine to sip and a nap to be had? Spain has perfected the art of slowing down time itself, proving that when you're in good company (or have wine), waiting feels less like a problem and more like a lifestyle.

The Spanish Art of "We'll Get to It"

Nowhere is Spain's effortless relationship with time more evident than in its legendary dining culture. While other countries rush through meals as if they're competing in an Olympic speed-eating event, Spain has turned dinner into a four-hour social marathon—complete with endless courses, unsolicited life advice from the waiter, and passionate debates about fútbol that could theoretically last until sunrise. If you thought you were just grabbing a quick bite, congratulations—you've now made lifelong friends with the entire staff and will likely be invited to someone's cousin's wedding.

And let's talk about *ferias*, Spain's legendary festivals, where time truly ceases to exist. A parade scheduled for noon? Good luck seeing movement before 3 p.m. A flamenco performance set to start "soon"? Go ahead and settle in with another glass of Rioja. Spaniards don't just wait—they stretch time, mold it, and turn it into a party. By the time things actually start, you've stopped caring about when it was supposed to happen, and you're too busy dancing in the streets to worry about it.

The Only Thing That Runs on Time: The Jamón

Spain may not be in a rush, but there is one exception: jamón ibérico. This perfectly cured ham, sliced so thin it's practically translucent, is treated with more reverence than some religious relics. Spaniards will happily spend years aging a leg of jamón to perfection, but the moment it's placed on the table, watch out—there is no waiting. You hesitate for even a second, and an abuela with lightning-fast reflexes will have already snagged the best piece. Turns out, Spain *can* be fast—when it really matters.

In Spain, time isn't something to conquer; it's something to enjoy. Whether it's a three-hour lunch, a festival that defies all schedules, or a siesta that turns into a full-on hibernation, waiting here isn't a nuisance—it's an invitation to savor life. Because in Spain, what's the rush? The world will still be spinning *mañana*.

In Spain, time bends to the will of good food, great company, and the occasional impromptu street parade. Meanwhile, over in Greece, waiting is more than a way of life—it's a full-blown dramatic performance, complete with expressive hand gestures, passionate sighs, and the occasional philosophical debate about why everything takes so damn long. Go on and pop in those noise-canceling earbuds, because we're about to turn the volume up on waiting.

Greece: Waiting with Passion, Drama, and Possibly a Plate of Baklava

Finally, we land in Greece, where waiting is not done quietly—it's done with passion, volume, and enough hand gestures to qualify as an Olympic sport. Greeks don't just wait; they perform. A minor delay? That's not an inconvenience—it's an affront to the gods. Complaining is not only encouraged—it's an art form. The sighs are theatrical, the eye-rolls nearly airborne, and the muttered curses? Poetic. You don't just voice your frustration—you share it with the entire square. And yet, somehow, through all the animated outrage, Greeks have also mastered the art of loving the wait just as much as they loathe it.

For all the expressive frustration, Greeks know how to lean into the wait with a kind of effortless, Zorba-the-Greek joy. Waiting for your coffee? That's an opportunity—to chat, debate, people-watch, and possibly fall into an impromptu philosophical discussion about the meaning of life. Lines at the post office? Perfect time to make new friends, trade life stories, and loudly discuss whose *yiayia* makes the best moussaka.

The Greek Time Warp

In Greece, time is a flexible concept, best understood in the context of *avrio* (tomorrow) or *methavrio* (the day after tomorrow). I wish everyone had a single word for the day after tomorrow how cool is that. If something doesn't happen today, no problem—it wasn't meant to happen today. Deadlines are suggestions, schedules are open to interpretation, and the best-laid plans are often replaced by spontaneous invitations to drink ouzo by the sea.

Tourists often arrive expecting efficiency and instead find themselves waiting 45 minutes for a waiter who is in no rush to take their order. But here's the secret: the waiter isn't ignoring you—he's giving you time. Time to sit, to relax, to just exist without rushing to the next thing. And if you try to wave him down in a hurry? Congratulations, you've just outed yourself as a non-Greek.

A National Love Affair with Life

For all the sighing, the complaining, the expressive frustration—deep down, waiting in Greece is really just an extension of their love affair with life itself. They refuse to rush through moments that deserve to be felt, tasted, and fully lived. This is a country where meals last for hours, conversations stretch until dawn, and a "quick coffee" is a social event requiring multiple rounds and possibly a full meal.

Imagine this: you're sitting at a taverna, sipping an ouzo so strong it could wake the gods, watching the world go by. A waiter strolls past—no rush. The table next to you erupts in laughter, an old man gestures wildly as he tells a story that will probably take another half-hour to finish. The sun is setting, your glass of ouzo is still half-full, and for once in a very long while, you don't care how long anything takes.

The Grand Tour Takeaway

So that concludes our global crash course in waiting like a pro (hope you took notes, America). At the end of the day, waiting is a universal truth—as inevitable as your cat knocking something off the table just to make deadpan eye contact while doing it. But suffering through it? That part's optional. Whether you queue like a Brit, vibe through it like a Jamaican, or turn it into a passionate *telenovela* like a Greek, there's always a way to make waiting work for you. And if all else fails? Just take a deep breath, order another coffee, and remember—*avrio* or methavrio are always good options. Balance, my friends. Life's too short to let waiting get the best of you.

Chapter Six

Mind the Time Gap

"Ain't it funny how time slips away?"
– Willie Nelson, *Funny How Time Slips Away*
(Not when you're staring at the clock, Willie.)

And so, dear reader, we return from our global quest with a truth as universal as time itself: waiting is what you make of it. Whether it's *lagom*, *hygge*, silence, noodles, or a theatrical Greek rant, other countries remind us that the wait isn't always the enemy. But why does waiting feel so different depending on where you are? Is it cultural? Philosophical? Or—brace yourself—could it be physics? In this section, we'll dive deep into the weird and wonderful world of time: its philosophy, its physics, and why waiting might just be the key to understanding both.

Time, the Ultimate Tease

If waiting is the art, time is the canvas—and what a strange, unreliable canvas it is. One moment it's crawling slower than a DMV line on a Monday morning; the next, it's sprinting like Usain Bolt when you're late for a flight. How is it that the same unit—a second, a minute, an hour—can stretch or shrink depending on our perception, our mood, or whether we're stuck listening to someone describe their dream in excruciating detail?

To understand waiting, we need to grapple with the beast itself: *time*. What is it? Why does it mess with us so much? And is waiting—that eternal pause—our best shot at unraveling its mysteries?

Time, Philosophically Speaking

Let's begin with the thinkers who have spent entire lifetimes contemplating time—a feat that seems both fitting and ironic. If you want to feel completely lost about the concept of time, philosophers have you covered.

Aristotle's Hot Take: If You Hate Waiting, Maybe You're Just Morally Inferior

Philosophers throughout history have grappled with the concept of waiting. Aristotle spoke of patience as the ability to endure hardship while maintaining virtue, a hallmark of moral excellence. The ancient Greeks distinguished between *kairos* (the opportune moment) and *chronos* (linear time), suggesting that waiting isn't merely about passing the time—it's about recognizing the right time.

So, according to Aristotle, if you despise waiting, you're not just impatient—you're morally suspect.

Which is great news for everyone who's ever yelled "Oh, come on!" at a traffic light. While others simply waited, the Greeks turned time into a concept worth overthinking for centuries. Recognizing the right moment to act, to move, to wait. And that's where things get even deeper, because if Aristotle thought patience made you virtuous, Simone Weil took it a step further. To her, waiting wasn't just a skill—it was a full-blown spiritual discipline.

Simone Weil: The Patron Saint of Holding for the Divine

For those inclined to find meaning in the agony, existentialist Simone Weil saw waiting as an act of attention, a way of connecting deeply with the present moment. Weil, often referred to as one of the most underappreciated patron saints of waiting, believed that patience wasn't passive—it was a form of active engagement with life's unfolding mysteries. To her, waiting was a spiritual exercise, akin to opening a door to the universe and standing still, allowing the vastness of existence to walk through.

And, oh, the weight of her insights! Weil famously said, "Waiting patiently in expectation is the foundation of the spiritual life." It's the kind of statement that makes you reconsider every time you've checked your phone in a line at Starbucks. If Simone Weil had been alive today, she might've turned a buffering Netflix screen into a TED Talk about grace under pressure. You can almost imagine her telling us, "Stop refreshing that delivery tracker. The universe will unfold its packages when it's damned good and ready."

Her life, marked by incredible intellect, deep compassion, and a relentless quest for truth, was no stranger to waiting. In her writing, you sense that waiting wasn't a delay—it was the point. It was through waiting that she uncovered the depth of her faith, her humanity, and her connection to the eternal. And if that isn't worth considering while you're stuck in traffic, what is?

Zeno's Paradox: Why You'll Never Reach the Front of the Queue

The ancient Greek philosopher Zeno had a thought experiment: you can never actually reach your destination because you must first get halfway there, then halfway of that halfway, and so on. It's like being stuck in the slowest-moving grocery store line—you inch forward but never seem to arrive. Zeno might've been onto something—because if you've ever waited in a grocery store line with one register open while the self-checkout machines mock you with their 'unexpected item in bagging area' nonsense, you know movement is an illusion.

Heraclitus: Time is Shit's Creek, and You Forgot Your Paddle

Heraclitus had one big idea: everything is always changing. He looked at time and basically said, "Good luck holding onto anything, because it's already slipping through your fingers." His famous line—"You can't step into the same river twice"—wasn't just poetic, it was a warning: time moves forward whether you like it or not.

But let's be real, if time is a river, it's not some peaceful babbling brook. It's more like whitewater rapids where you lost the oars, dropped your phone in the water, and now a very judgmental fish is watching you flail. Try to grab onto a moment, and whoosh—it's gone. Try to pause time, and the current will just drag you along anyway. It's why nostalgia hits so hard. It's why waiting feels so long when you want it to speed up and so short when you want it to last.

And while we're at it—why does no one ever talk about what happens if you *do* step into the same river twice? Presumably, your shoes are soaked, and now you're just some guy standing in a river, pondering existence while a confused duck floats by.

Saint Augustine: The Original "It's Complicated"

Then along came Augustine of Hippo, who famously wrote, "What then is time? If no one asks me, I know what it is. If I wish to explain it to him who asks, I do not know." Which is a fancy way of saying, *I totally get time until someone asks me to explain it, and then my brain melts.* Essentially, he was the guy at the party who seemed really deep until you realized he just talked in circles until everyone else gave up.

Augustine believed that time wasn't some external force—it was something happening in our own minds. The past? Just a memory. The future? Just anticipation. The present? Already slipping away as you try to pin it down. Basically, he turned time into a metaphysical prank: the moment you try to grab it, *poof*—it's gone. If he were around today, he'd probably describe it as trying to cancel a free trial one second before it auto-renews.

Immanuel Kant: Time Is Just a Glitch in Your Brain's Software

Don't even get me started on Kant. He argued that time isn't some grand, universal force ticking away in the cosmos—it's just something our brains invented to make sense of reality. Basically, time is a feature in the human mind's operating system, and like all software, it sometimes lags, crashes, or makes you feel like your DoorDash driver has been *out for delivery* for the past seven years. Thanks, brain.

Kant would say that waiting isn't real in any absolute sense—it's just your perception stretching and warping time like a funhouse mirror. When you're binge-watching your favorite show, time is zipping around like a mosquito in a nudist colony. But when you're stuck in traffic, every minute drags slower than paint drying on a humid day. Kant would probably argue that waiting is just the brain throwing a tantrum because it expected to be somewhere else already. If he were alive today, he'd be the guy sitting in a therapist's waiting room, staring into the middle distance, whispering to himself, *None of this is real*.

Philosophers vs. Time: A Cage Match That Never Ends

All this to say: philosophically speaking, time is confusing, and waiting forces us to confront that confusion head-on. It's like holding up a mirror to time itself and saying, *"Oh, I see what you're doing here, you sneaky bastard."*

And that's why philosophers have spent centuries wrestling with it—because nothing says *fun* like questioning whether time is real while waiting for your soup to cool. Some, like Aristotle, tried to make sense of it. Others, like Zeno, turned it into a paradox just to mess with people. Augustine basically threw up his hands and said, *"Time? Oh yeah, easy. It's—wait, no. Hold on. Okay, give me a second. No, wait, that's time too… Damn it."* And according to our buddy Kant, that agonizing three-hour meeting was just a mental construct. Fantastic. Tell that to my ass Kant, which fell asleep in the first twenty minutes.

So what's the takeaway? That waiting is *deeply* philosophical, and if you ever find yourself stuck in a long, excruciating line, just tell yourself: *Ah yes, I am engaging in a rich intellectual tradition.* Or, if that doesn't help, just start whispering "None of this is real" and see if you can freak out the person next to you.

If you thought philosophers were confusing, wait until you meet the physicists. You might want to sit down for this part, preferably with paper bag to breathe into.

Einstein Walks Into the DMV

Einstein walks into a DMV. Three hours later, he walks out a broken man, muttering, *"Time is relative, but this is fucking ridiculous."*

Let's start with Einstein, because duh, of course. Einstein's theory of relativity blew everyone's minds by proving that time is not fixed—it's stretchy, bendy, and totally at the mercy of speed and gravity. He taught us that time is relative. Sure, he was talking about astronauts traveling near the speed of light, but it's just as applicable to standing in line at the DMV.

Time slows down when you're near massive objects, like black holes...or a government office so dense with inefficiency that light can't escape. A single minute at the DMV somehow lasts an hour, while an hour with friends passes in a flash. That's relativity, my friends. It's not your imagination—physics is literally working against you. You walk into the DMV at noon. You check your watch—it's still noon. You check again—it's still noon. Einstein nods. 'Told ya.'

Time Dilation: Explains Black Holes, DMV Lines, and Your Grandma's Stories
Because nothing bends time like government paperwork and a tale that starts with, "Back in my day..."

So to recap, move fast enough or hang out near a black hole, and time slows down. Yes, this means if you spent your afternoon traveling at near-light speed, you'd experience less time than your friend who spent the same afternoon binge-watching Netflix.

This is called time dilation, and it's proof that waiting is not only psychological—it's physical. That 20-minute wait for your dentist appointment? Depending on where you are in the universe, it might feel like five minutes... or 500 years. The faster you move, the slower you age. This means that if you're stuck in traffic and not moving, you're technically aging faster. So the next time you're sitting bumper-to-bumper, just think of it as a quantum nudge to carpool more often.

To wrap things up, the laws of physics always have your back my friend, so next time someone accuses you of exaggerating how long you've been waiting, just whisper, "Einstein."

The Arrow of Time: Why Waiting Always Moves Forward

According to physics, time moves in one direction because of entropy, the universe's tendency toward disorder. Think of a neatly stacked grocery aisle turning into chaos after a toddler rampages through it. Time flows forward because entropy increases, which also explains why the coffee you spilled five minutes ago isn't cleaning itself up. Waiting taps into this idea of entropy—it feels like time itself is unraveling the longer you're stuck in line.

But here's a comforting thought: the arrow of time means every wait will eventually end. Whether it's the barista calling your name or the traffic light finally turning green, the universe is contractually obligated to keep moving forward...eventually.

In quantum physics, time gets even weirder. On a subatomic level, particles behave in ways that seem to defy time entirely—moving backward, forward, or appearing to exist in multiple places at once. So technically, your Uber Eats driver is both 'arriving soon' and lost on the other side of town at the same time. Uh, thanks I guess... Quantum mechanics? That's right: the universe is out there pulling a *Doctor Strange* while you're stuck waiting. The takeaway? Time is slippery. It doesn't always behave the way we think it should, and waiting—that feeling of time dragging its feet—might just be our best clue that time isn't as straightforward as it seems.

Smartphones: The Ultimate Time Machine

If time is a construct, then smartphones are the tools we use to deconstruct it. Stuck waiting? Pull out your phone. Now you're not simply waiting; you're scrolling, swiping, and refreshing.

Smartphones have turned waiting into a semi-productive activity. You can answer emails, watch TikToks, or doom-scroll your way through any wait. Suddenly time magically disappears. One second, you're checking one email. The next, you've watched twelve cat videos, accidentally shopped for a kayak, and it's two hours later. If time is an illusion, smartphones are the greatest magicians of all.

The Illusion of Time (Or, Why Einstein Would Laugh at Your Pizza Tracker)

So where does waiting fit into all this? Well, for starters, it proves just how unreliable our experience of time actually is. When you're waiting, you feel every second stretch like an overworked rubber band. Your brain is in hyper-awareness mode, tracking time like a nosy neighbor who just *knows* the HOA rules are being broken. Meanwhile, physics tells us time isn't as straightforward as we think—meaning your frustration over a "late" DoorDash driver might be less about delay and more about your brain straight-up gaslighting you.

This disconnect between how time actually works and how we experience it is part of what makes waiting so maddening. The human mind was not built to deal with time dilation, quantum uncertainty, or the fact that clocks tick slightly slower on airplanes than they do on Earth. But here we are, furiously refreshing tracking links as if sheer willpower can force Amazon Prime to warp spacetime.

Waiting forces us to confront the fact that time isn't fixed—it's a slippery little bastard that bends, stretches, and warps depending on how we interact with it. And when you realize that, suddenly, waiting shifts from mere annoyance to a front-row seat to the strangeness of the universe.

Time: Universe's Most Passive-Aggressive Prank

You're not simply waiting—you're participating in one of the greatest mysteries of the universe. And sure, it's frustrating, but it's also a little bit wonderful. After all, what's the rush? Time's going to do its thing whether you like it or not.

And if you happen to be reading this while waiting for something... congratulations. You've just used that time to contemplate the nature of time itself, making you and Einstein practically buddies. Not bad for a pause, eh?

The universe doesn't just mess with time—it lets *you* do it, too. Why does time drag when you're bored? Why does waiting seem longer when you're anxious? And what happens in your brain, your body, and your very cells when you're stuck in that eternal pause? It's time to uncover the psychology, physiology, and neuroscience of waiting—because it turns out, time isn't only bending around black holes; it's twisting inside your head, too.

It's All in Your Head: The Neuroscience of Waiting

So, in Physics, we've learned that time is flexible, weird, and probably messing with us on purpose. But if time is the universe's wild card, our perception of time is the sneaky dealer stacking the deck. Waiting—that feeling of time dragging its feet—has less to do with physics and more to do with psychology, physiology, and neuroscience.

In other words, it's all in your head.

The Psychology of Waiting: Why Does Time Slow Down When You're Bored?

Let's start with the obvious: time flies when you're having fun, and it crawls when you're not. Why? The answer is in your brain's relationship with novelty and focus.

When you're engaged in something exciting—a thrilling conversation, a roller coaster ride, a Netflix marathon—your brain doesn't bother to track every passing second. It's too busy soaking up the experience. But when you're waiting, your brain... notices. It notices *everything*. The ticking clock. The humming light. The unsettlingly enthusiastic nostril breathing of the person next to you. Without distractions, your brain turns into a chaos generator—counting ceiling tiles, fixating on whether it's been you breathing weird this whole time, or developing an irrational hatred for the way that one guy chews like a deranged forest animal.

Psychologists call this the time-awareness paradox. The more you pay attention to time, the longer it feels. It's as if your brain is punishing you for not being entertained.

The solution? Distract your brain. Join the Borg and stare at your phone. Or, if you're like me, spend the next five minutes debating whether the guy in front of you is a lizard person struggling to blend in or a serial killer whose only mistake (so far) was pairing dress shoes with ankle socks. Verdict: unsure. Anything to keep from staring at the clock.

The Psychology of Perceived Wait Times

Studies show that people are more willing to wait if they feel like their time isn't being wasted. This is why restaurants give you pagers or why apps show you progress bars—it's not just about the actual wait, but how it feels. By offering transparency, distractions, or small rewards (hello, free breadsticks!), businesses can turn a frustrating experience into a tolerable one.

The Physiology of Waiting: Your Body on Hold

But waiting doesn't just mess with your head—it messes with your body, too. Ever notice how being late for an appointment stuck in traffic makes your heart rate tick up, your palms sweat, or your muscles tense? That's your body hitting the fight-or-flight button, even though there's nothing to fight and nowhere to fly.

When you're stuck waiting—especially if it's unexpected or stressful—your brain triggers the release of cortisol, the stress hormone. This is your body's way of preparing for action, even if the only action you can take is shuffling a little closer to the front of the line. Over time, chronic waiting (think airport delays, long commutes, or mind-numbing hold music) can leave you feeling drained, anxious, or even physically exhausted.

The Neuroscience of Waiting: Why Your Brain Hates Delays

Neuroscientists have found that waiting lights up the parts of your brain associated with the need for pursuit of reward, anticipation, and frustration. Delays disrupt your brain's dopamine cycle—that feel-good chemical you get when things go as planned. When you expect something to happen (your food to arrive, the light to turn green) and it doesn't, your dopamine levels drop, and you feel let down. Your brain, in essence, throws a tiny tantrum.

Chronic stress from feeling like the universe owes you instant gratification spikes cortisol levels, which in turn can lead to high blood pressure, heart disease, and a strong urge to yell at inanimate objects. Even at a genetic level, waiting might accelerate aging: research from the National Institutes of Health suggests that chronic stress shortens telomeres, the protective caps on chromosomes, potentially reducing lifespan. So, in a cruel twist of irony, the more we demand instant results, the faster we're running out of time. How fun!

But here's the thing: studies show that the anticipation of something good—like waiting for vacation or a birthday—can actually be *more rewarding* than the thing itself. Your brain loves the build-up. So maybe waiting isn't all bad. There's a certain magic in anticipation, like the universe winking at you and saying, "Just wait... you're gonna love this."

Every wait is an unintentional science experiment—your brain vs. boredom, with absolutely no referee. The wait may seem like it's taking forever and a day, but it's your brain playing tricks on you. So breathe. Distract yourself. Maybe even enjoy the wait. Because when you understand what's happening in your head, waiting starts to feel a little less maddening—and a little more fascinating.

Time, Waiting, and the Great Cosmic Joke

Well, we've covered a ton of ground in this chapter: philosophy, physics, neuroscience, basically everything short of consulting a psychic or shaking a Magic 8-Ball.

So, what have we learned? Time is a slippery little trickster. Philosophers can't define it, physicists can't pin it down, and neuroscientists say your brain is making half of the shit up anyway. Waiting forces us to confront time in all its weirdness—how it bends, stretches, warps, and occasionally mocks us at the DMV. But maybe that's the whole point. Maybe waiting isn't something we suffer through—it's the universe's way of making us actually notice time instead of just burning through it.

For all this deep contemplation, waiting still *feels* like a pain in the ass sometimes. Sure, it's a philosophical exercise, a quantum mystery, and a neurological experiment, but it's also that thing that makes you rage-text customer service at 3 a.m. Because waiting isn't only about patience—it has real consequences. Missed opportunities. Delayed gratification. Lost time we'll never get back. And in a world that runs on speed, waiting comes with a price tag.

In the next chapter, we'll take a look at the costs of waiting, exploring how delays impact us in ways both big and small.

Not the eco-heroic waiting but the soul sucking frustrating kind. When you're stuck in traffic, or in a long line, waiting can feel like life's cruelest tax stealing your time, energy, and even your health. Because while patience may be a virtue, it often comes with a big price tag.

Part III

The Cost of Waiting

Chapter Seven

The Price Is Not Right: The Cost of Waiting

"Time is on my side... yes, it is."
 The Rolling Stones, *Time Is on My Side*
(*Actually, Mick, time is on no one's side. The IRS and my internet provider have confirmed this.*)

Let's face it: waiting can kinda suck sometimes. It's the broccoli of life—we know it's good for us, but we'd rather binge on the deep-fried dopamine rush of instant results. Under the surface there is a truth no one wants to admit: waiting is more than just inconvenient—it's an economic and emotional battlefield. More cars on the road, more stress in our minds, and (brace yourself) possibly more divisiveness in society. Could our refusal to wait be fueling not only road rage, but also culture wars? Buckle up buttercup, because this rabbit hole goes deep and it's traffic-jammed.

The Economics of Waiting: Time Is Money, and Stress Costs Extra

Picture your average traffic jam. It's rush hour; you're sitting in a metal box, burning gas, and calculating how many snacks you have before resorting to cannibalism? If you drive 30 minutes to and from work daily, you spend 125 hours a year just waiting. That's over five days each year spent fuming because some guy in an SUV can't merge properly.

This isn't simply a personal annoyance; it's a massive economic drain. Traffic congestion costs the U.S. economy about $87 billion annually in wasted fuel and lost productivity. And that's before we factor in the cost of road rage therapy or the number of stress-eating bags of Funyuns consumed during these delays. The economic impact of waiting isn't limited to cars, either. On hold, in lines, time might be money, but impatience is the price you pay.

Stress and the Short Fuse Epidemic

Now let's quickly review what we learned in the last chapter about what all this waiting is doing to our brains. Prolonged stress—like the kind induced by sitting in traffic or watching your Uber driver make inexplicable turns—activates our amygdala, the brain's emotional command center. The result? Higher levels of cortisol, the stress hormone that turns us from rational adults into toddlers who missed nap time.

Waiting erodes our patience like a vending machine that eats your dollar and pretends it never met you, making us more likely to snap at coworkers, family members, or random strangers who dare to exist in our line of sight. Stress-induced impatience creates a ripple effect: the angry honk in traffic becomes a snippy email, which becomes a passive-aggressive social media post, which snowballs into a full-blown Facebook rant about how "people these days" are walking proof that evolution might've hit the brakes.

Waiting and the Anxiety Feedback Loop

Here's where it gets deep (and a little weird): impatience isn't simply a side effect of stress—it's fueling even more impatience. The less we wait, the worse we get at it. Think about it: we've built a world where you can order groceries, stream a movie, and book therapy—all without getting off your couch. And yet, despite all this convenience, anxiety levels are skyrocketing. Coincidence? Maybe. But what if, in trying to remove all the waiting, we've just made ourselves more miserable when it fate-slaps us anyway?

When we can't cope with small frustrations, we're more vulnerable to bigger ones. The slow cashier becomes a personal affront. The differing opinion becomes a melodramatic threat. The inability to reconcile with waiting—for traffic to clear, for conflict to resolve, for understanding to emerge—breeds a culture where we're always on edge, always ready to pick a fight.

The Divisiveness Hypothesis: Is Impatience Tearing Us Apart?

Now, here's the wild part. What if our inability to wait isn't only making us stressed, but also more divided? Think about it: impatience thrives on binary thinking. It's the mental equivalent of a fast-food menu—we want clear options, served quickly, with no room for nuance. But real life is more like a slow-cooked stew. It takes time, patience, and a willingness to let flavors (or ideas) simmer.

When we're impatient, we're less likely to engage in thoughtful dialogue. We want instant agreement, not messy conversations. This mindset doesn't just affect our personal lives; it's a recipe for societal division. Think of any hot-button issue—politics, climate change, healthcare, pineapple on pizza. The more impatient we are, the less we're willing to wait for understanding, compromise, or middle ground. And the more divided we become.

The Waiting Tax: Your Day, Your Life, The World

Have you ever stopped to consider how much of your life is spent waiting? From the daily drag of drive-thru lines that move at the speed of erosion to the bureaucratic black hole of the DMV, where efficiency is just a rumor and patience is the only accepted form of currency. Waiting has a way of whittling down your patience, leaving you clinging to your last shred of sanity like a frayed rope. Imagine if every second lost to waiting had a dollar amount attached—would we be rich or just really, really bitter? Waiting is everywhere in our daily lives like the Final Jeopardy song playing in a loop—cheerfully mocking us with its doo-doo-doo as we scramble to fill the silence. Imagine that multiplied by a lifetime.

The Hidden Cost of Waiting

A little waiting here, a little waiting there—no big deal, right? Well, let's add it up:

- Morning Coffee Line: 7 minutes wasted while the guy ahead debates oat milk vs. almond milk.
- Traffic on the Commute: 25 minutes of brake lights and deep theatrical sighing.
- Lunch Rush: 18 minutes between ordering and watching your avocado toast arrive with suspiciously brown edges.
- Meetings That Should Have Been Emails: 12 minutes waiting for Brenda to unmute herself.
- Grocery Checkout: 11 minutes stuck behind someone who just *now* decided to sign up for the store rewards program.

Total daily waiting: 73 minutes.
That's over 19 full workdays a year. Just... gone.

So..., we get an average 2 weeks vacation a year from our employer and spend 3 weeks a year in traffic driving to and from work. Hmm....Tell me again why no one is saying anything about this?

Now let's talk money. If time is worth about $30 an hour, that's $13,000 a year down the drain—enough to take a dream vacation, buy a secondhand sports car, or, ironically, hire someone to wait in every line for you.

And over a lifetime? We're talking four whole years spent waiting—as if the universe decided to grant you a free Bachelors degree in *Standing Around Doing Nothing*. Oh, and the financial cost? Over $300,000 worth of your time—poof. That's a house, a retirement fund, or the world's longest five-star vacation, lost to red lights, buffering screens, and hold music that should be classified as psychological torture.

Now, take that one wasted hour a day, multiply it by all 330 million people in America, and slap a $30 per hour price tag on it. Over a year, that's a mind-melting $3.6 trillion—roughly the entire GDP of the United Kingdom. That's enough to buy all 8 million people in London a brand-new Rolls-Royce—and still have millions left over to gold-plate the streets of Mayfair.

The Big Picture

Zooming out, this isn't simply an *us* problem—it's a *humanity* problem. If everyone on the planet loses even an hour a day to waiting, that's millions of years of collective time vanishing into the void, every single day. Productivity lost. Energy drained. Lives spent standing in line instead of *actually living*.

So yeah—waiting isn't just annoying. It's expensive AF, exhausting, and possibly the greatest heist of human potential we've ever pulled on ourselves.

But what if it didn't have to be this way?

Now that we've established that waiting is a global parasite feasting on our time, money, and sanity, it's natural to crave a way out. What if waiting wasn't just a burden we begrudgingly endure but something we could outsmart, minimize, or even transform?

Sadly, solutions don't just fall from the sky (though wouldn't that be convenient?). The path to fixing our waiting woes is a journey that we'll dive into all of that later in this book, where solutions await. But for now, let's sit with the weight of the problem a little longer—because understanding the cost is the first step toward change.

Conclusion: The Revolution Awaits

Waiting may be the great equalizer but it doesn't have to be the great oppressor. With a little cooperation and innovation we can reclaim our time and reshape the way we live. The solutions might seem far-fetched, but so did self-driving cars and robot vacuums once. So why not dream big?

After all, the future isn't going to wait for us—so let's stop waiting for it.

So if waiting is unfair, the obvious solution is to eliminate it, right? Just speed everything up—cut the lines, overnight the packages, summon a car at the push of a button.

Well, *not so fast* (literally). Because while skipping the wait might feel like a win, it turns out that all this instant gratification comes at a cost—a massive, fuel-guzzling, air-choking cost. Every express delivery, every single-item shipment, every time you demand something *right now* instead of *next week*? The planet picks up the tab. And it's not cheap.

In the next chapter, we're pulling back the curtain on the high price of speed—how our addiction to convenience is reshaping not just our expectations, but the atmosphere itself. Because as it turns out, waiting a little longer might be one of the easiest ways to help save the world.

Chapter Eight

The Carbon Cost of Convenience

"Running on empty."
– Jackson Browne, Running on Empty
(Because nothing says "sustainability" like express shipping a single tube of ChapStick.)

Convenience has gone from luxury to expectation. One tap, and your latest 'must-have' is en route—sometimes arriving so quickly, you're still trying to remember why you ordered it. But let's talk about the fine print. Behind the scenes, this lightning-fast delivery system comes with an environmental price tag big enough to make even the most optimistic climate scientists reach for a stress ball.

Same-Day Shipping: The Carbon Culprit

When you click "Buy Now," a chain reaction begins. Warehouses spring into action, trucks hit the road, and planes take off—all to ensure your Bluetooth-enabled banana slicer arrives yesterday. But all this urgency doesn't just burn through your savings; it guzzles fuel like it's auditioning for a role in a Fast & Furious spin-off.

Studies show that same-day shipping can produce up to 50% more carbon emissions per package compared to standard shipping. Why? Because rush deliveries often bypass optimized routes, meaning half-empty trucks and planes crisscross the country like caffeinated squirrels. It's logistics gone wild, and the planet pays the price.

Now, let's zoom in on air travel—not the kind where you're uncomfortably squished between a snorer and a screaming toddler, but the cargo flights that make your overnight shipping dreams come true. Aviation already accounts for about 2.5% of global carbon dioxide emissions, and freight planes are the bad boys of the skies. They burn nearly 10 times more fuel per ton-mile than trains. So while your next-day delivery is flying high, so are our global temperatures.

And don't think ground transport gets a free pass. Those zippy delivery vans that buzz around your neighborhood? They're like the bees of consumerism, except instead of pollinating flowers, they're belching out CO_2. Studies show that last-mile deliveries—the final stretch from distribution center to your doorstep—are responsible for about 53% of a shipment's total emissions. That's a lot of pollution for the sake of getting your sourdough starter kit before brunch.

Streaming: The Invisible Carbon Stream

But it's not just delivery services contributing to our collective carbon footprint. Streaming your favorite shows feels guilt-free, but giant data centers are chugging away behind the scenes, guzzling electricity like frat boys at a keg party. In fact, the internet accounts for about 2% of global carbon emissions, rivaling the aviation industry.

Here's a fun fact to help put that into perspective: Watching one hour of Netflix emits about as much CO_2 as driving 0.14 miles, which is roughly the length of a city block. So while your love of true crime shows isn't exactly criminal, binging an entire season in a weekend might earn you some side-eye from an eco-conscious polar bear.

Even our need for faster internet has environmental consequences. The infrastructure required to deliver high-speed connectivity—think satellites, fiber-optic cables, and 5G towers—demands a huge amount of energy and resources. All so you can stream cat videos without buffering.

Waiting for Greatness: A Hypothetical Thought Experiment

Let's talk about the cost of waiting—not the DMV variety, but the kind that makes you contemplate moving to a remote cabin and communicating solely by carrier pigeon. Let's paint an unrealistic worst-case scenario—just to make a point: the entire world (yes, all 8 billion of us) hops into gas-guzzling SUVs every day, commuting 10 miles each way to work. Then, we click "Buy Now" on everything—coffee, cat litter, that gadget we'll never use—each item arriving in its own giant box, non-consolidated, because why not maximize the environmental guilt?

The result? Global CO_2 emissions would skyrocket far beyond today's 36.3 billion metric tons annually. Let's break it down:

Daily Commutes: If all 8 billion of us drove 20 miles round-trip to work in gas SUVs, this alone would generate 16.2 billion metric tons of CO_2 per year.

Non-Consolidated Shipping: Add another 8 billion metric tons annually from single-item deliveries, where every purchase is boxed, shipped, and transported separately.

Together, this would push global emissions to a staggering 60.5 billion metric tons per year—a 67% increase over today. At this rate, we would burn through the carbon budget for +4°C warming in around 66 years, making life as we know it vastly more dangerous, with large swaths of the planet uninhabitable.

A wake-up call? Sure. But the good news is this story isn't set in stone, it's scribbled in emissions, and we've got the eraser.

Slow Down, Save the World

So, what's the alternative? Patience. (Not glamorous, I know.) Choosing standard shipping can cut emissions by up to 50%. Ordering everything at once instead of in a million boxes? Also helps. And maybe—you don't actually need to buy that thing at all. Crazy, right?

Our obsession with speed isn't inherently bad—it's brought incredible advancements in technology, medicine, and global connectivity. But when speed comes at the expense of sustainability, it's time to rethink our priorities. The goal shouldn't be to eliminate waiting entirely; it should be to align our desire for convenience with the planet's capacity to keep up.

A lot of this environmental carnage is completely avoidable. Research indicates that nearly 40% of consumers admit they don't actually need their orders immediately. That's right, nearly half of us are clicking "Rush Delivery" out of sheer impatience or boredom. Let's be real—is it really worth accelerating the heat death of the planet for a set of novelty socks?

As consumers, we have more power than we think. By making small, intentional choices—opting for slower shipping, supporting sustainable businesses, and embracing the occasional wait—we can reduce our environmental impact without giving up modern conveniences entirely.

Let's reframe waiting as an act of eco-heroism. Every time you resist the urge to upgrade shipping, you're basically Captain Planet with a credit card. Plus, waiting can be good for you. It builds character. It teaches you gratitude. And most importantly, it gives you more time to write hilariously angry reviews about how slow the delivery was.

The next time you're tempted by same-day shipping, ask yourself: do I want this now, or do I want the planet to exist later? If you pick the latter, congratulations—you're not only a consumer but officially a world-saving legend in the making. Now go forth and save the world, one delayed package at a time.

Small Changes, Big Impact

You don't need to overhaul your entire life to make a difference. A few small changes can collectively add up to a big win for the planet:

The Fridge List: Keep a running list for Amazon, Walmart, or Target orders. Place one consolidated order at the end of the week instead of five separate ones. Your fridge has been prepping you for this your whole life.

Standard Shipping: Opt for no-rush delivery whenever possible. Not only will you reduce emissions, but you might earn a discount or reward. Saving the planet and your wallet? Win-win.

Local Love: Shop at nearby farmers' markets or independent stores. Your lettuce doesn't need frequent flyer miles. Bonus points if you bike there.

Streaming Breaks: Commit to binging responsibly. One episode per night doesn't just stretch out the enjoyment of a great series—it also reduces your carbon footprint.

Amazon and Walmart: Trying to Be Green Giants

Even the giants of convenience are trying to clean up their act. Amazon, for example, has pledged to go net-zero carbon by 2040, with plans to deploy 100,000 electric delivery vehicles by 2030. Over 20,000 of these EVs are already zipping around neighborhoods as of 2024, quietly reducing emissions while delivering your yoga mat.

Walmart, in a plot twist no one saw coming, has embraced sustainability by using stores as local fulfillment centers, reducing long-haul emissions. Their AI-driven delivery systems batch orders together like a carpool for your groceries. Imagine your frozen pizza, shampoo, and duct tape all hitching a ride together—talk about efficiency.

Other Companies Leading the Charge

Several other major corporations are also transitioning to electric vehicle (EV) fleets:

FedEx: Plans to have 50% of its new vehicle purchases be electric by 2025, 100% by 2030, and aims for its entire delivery fleet to be electric by 2040.

UPS: Has placed significant orders for EVs to replace internal combustion engine vehicles in its delivery fleet.

DHL: Aims to have more than 80,000 electric vehicles in its global fleet by 2030.

Slower, Smarter Systems: Lessons from Abroad

While Amazon, Walmart, and others are stepping up their sustainability game, other countries are already masters of the *slow and steady wins the planet* approach. Think of it as the tortoise teaching the hare how to recycle.

In Copenhagen, bike-powered cargo fleets zip through the streets delivering groceries and even furniture (yes, furniture!). According to a report from The European Cyclists' Federation, cargo bikes could replace up to 51% of urban delivery trips, significantly cutting emissions and congestion.

In Tokyo, the Takkyubin system—a delivery network so precise it borders on a science—consolidates packages for entire neighborhoods into single, optimized routes, reducing road traffic and emissions. According to Japan's Ministry of Land, Infrastructure, Transport, and Tourism, these efficiencies have helped lower last-mile delivery emissions by up to 40%. Customers can even schedule deliveries down to the hour or reroute them to nearby convenience stores, proving that logistics should adapt to people, not the other way around. Meanwhile, Germany's Paketboxen—shared neighborhood delivery lockers—have been shown in studies by Fraunhofer IML to reduce delivery truck stops by up to 30%, cutting emissions and encouraging neighbors to say, *Hallo!* a little more often.

Helsinki has taken a futuristic approach with autonomous electric buses, seamlessly transporting both people and packages. According to the Finnish Transport and Communications Agency, these self-driving shuttles have reduced emissions while integrating into public transit networks, easing urban congestion. Zurich's answer to traffic jams? Just skip the roads entirely, high above the Alps, Zurich's drones are busy delivering medical essentials to remote villages—sometimes hours away by road. A Swiss Post report found that drone deliveries in mountainous regions cut transport times by 80% while reducing emissions compared to traditional vehicle transport.

Stockholm, Sweden takes waste management so seriously that it built an underground vacuum-powered system to whisk garbage and recyclables straight to processing facilities. According to Envac, the Swedish company behind the system, this setup has reduced garbage truck traffic by 60% while converting organic waste into biogas. Yes, in Stockholm, even your banana peel can have a second career as fuel. Efficiency has never been so... *sucky*.

These cities aren't just proving that sustainable solutions exist—they're showing that we don't have to choose between convenience and saving the planet. But what if we took these ideas even further? What if, instead of just tweaking how we consume, we completely rethought the way we live and move through the world?

A Better-Case Scenario: A World Reimagined

Now let's imagine the opposite best-case scenario: What if those of us whose jobs allow for it worked remotely from home, avoiding daily commutes altogether? What if, instead of relying on gas-guzzling SUVs and non-consolidated shipping, we biked, walked, or peddled to local farmers markets with reusable bags in tow?

The pandemic proved we could do this. If 40% of workers stayed remote, the fallout wouldn't just be fewer traffic jams—it'd be a boom in efficiency, a drop in awkward watercooler small talk, and a world where "let's touch base" actually means getting stuff done.

Imagine: fewer cars clogging up the roads, smoother drives for those who still need to show up in person, and a major dent in transportation emissions. Think of all the honking and exhaust fumes replaced by birdsong and cleaner air. Add to that smarter shopping habits and a dash of local sourcing, and you've got a recipe for a much greener world. Suddenly, that commute-free lifestyle isn't only about working in pajama pants—it's a potential climate superhero move.

Sure, slashing global emissions from 36.3 billion metric tons to 6 billion might sound ambitious, but it's not as wild as it seems. Transportation alone is responsible for nearly a quarter of energy-related CO_2 emissions. Cutting down on commutes and tweaking our consumer habits could shave billions off those totals. And okay, maybe we won't hit an 83% reduction overnight, but the world would certainly breathe easier—literally.

With fewer emissions flooding the atmosphere, we might even get a little extra time on the carbon clock. Instead of burning through the carbon budget for a disastrous 4°C temperature rise in just over a century, we could stretch that timeline out by decades—critical years that could give us a fighting chance to implement real, sustainable change. The same goes for the dreaded +2°C threshold. Instead of racing toward it in a few decades, we could buy ourselves time to rein in the worst effects of climate change and maybe even keep polar bears from learning to surf.

And who knows? Given enough time, the Earth might even start cooling. All of this, because millions of people ditched their commutes, shopped a little smarter, and proved that fighting climate change doesn't always require grand gestures. Sometimes, it's as simple as staying home and making thoughtful choices.

The Power of Purposeful Waiting

Here's where waiting comes in: small acts of intentional waiting—like consolidating your shopping list into one weekly order—can have huge ripple effects. You wait a little longer for your groceries to arrive, but you're not stuck staring at an empty fridge.

And those small acts add up. Imagine billions of people biking instead of driving, shopping locally instead of relying on endless deliveries, and working remotely where possible. The best-case scenario isn't simply possible—it's joyful. Because guess what? Biking to the farmers market is fun. Knowing your neighbors is rewarding. And slowing down isn't a sacrifice; it's a chance to live better.

And the best part? You can make a positive difference, and all you have to do... is wait.

In the next chapter we switch gears. While we're out here making noble sacrifices like waiting an extra 48 hours for a new air fryer, the ultra-rich have taken a different approach: *buy the planet and turn it into an all-access VIP speed pass.* Why wait for anything when you can simply throw money at the problem until it disappears? Traffic? Fly over it. Crowds? Rent the place out. Public services? Privatize them and charge everyone else a fee. While we're standing here waiting, the 1% are already halfway to their private islands, sipping martinis made from the tears of people stuck in line.

Chapter Nine

A Tale of Two Lines: The Have-To's and the Wait-Not's

"You can't always get what you want."
The Rolling Stones
(*Unless you have a private jet, then waiting isn't even a concept you recognize.*)

Not all waiting is created equal. For some, waiting is a mild inconvenience. For others, it's a significant barrier to opportunity, productivity, and even survival. Welcome to the great waiting divide, where your place in line isn't just about patience—it's about your bank account, your zip code, and whether you can afford to press fast-forward.

The Geography of Waiting

Let's start with where you live. In rural areas, underfunded government services like DMVs often lead to long waits for something as simple as renewing a driver's license.

City folk, on the other hand, often deal with overcrowded public transit systems and endless traffic jams. Neither group is winning here, but the root causes differ: rural areas suffer from too few resources, while urban centers crack under the weight of too many people.

For those depending on public transportation, waiting isn't a nuisance—it's practically a second job. Late buses, missed connections, and infrequent service schedules can turn a 20-minute commute into a daily ordeal. A study in the U.S. found that people who rely on public transit spend an average of 150 more hours per year commuting than those who drive. That's almost an entire week lost just waiting for a ride.

In countries like India, waiting inequality takes on a stark form. Patients in rural areas often travel hours to access healthcare, only to spend the entire day waiting at under-resourced clinics. In urban slums, overcrowded public hospitals mean wait times for simple treatments like antibiotics can often stretch into weeks. This delay is more than inconvenient—it can be life-threatening.

Need a social grant or government service in South Africa? Be prepared to wait—sometimes for hours, sometimes in brutal weather, and sometimes at the cost of a day's wages. For many, waiting isn't just an inconvenience; it's a gamble with real financial stakes. And that's only the beginning. Geography is just one piece of the waiting puzzle. Even within the same city, the time tax isn't evenly applied. Because if there's one thing wealth can buy—besides faster Wi-Fi and better seats at a concert—it's the ability to skip the line entirely.

The Income Divide

If you've got money, waiting might as well be someone else's problem. The ultra-rich live in a world where they wait for nothing. Private jets eliminate airport delays, concierge medical services skip appointment backlogs, and exclusive memberships grant front-of-the-line access to everything from amusement parks to luxury resorts. Have you ever seen a billionaire standing in line at the DMV? Of course not. They probably have someone else handle it—or better yet, they've lobbied to privatize the service entirely.

The VIP Line to Life (And Why You're Not on the List)

For the rest of us, waiting isn't simply inconvenient; it's expensive. Lower-income individuals are more likely to endure long lines for essential services like healthcare, where Medicaid patients often face weeks-long waits for appointments compared to the near-instant access enjoyed by those with private insurance. Even grocery shopping comes with disparities: higher-income shoppers can afford delivery services, while others wait in line at overcrowded stores.

Waiting in Venezuela isn't about patience—it's about survival. With shortages everywhere, a simple grocery run can mean standing in line for hours, hoping there's still something left by the time you reach the front. The emotional toll is real, as parents anxiously hope there's still stock when it's their turn, knowing that one missed line could mean going hungry.

Waiting Inequality in Action

The numbers don't lie—where you live and how much money you have dictate how long you wait. And while waiting in line for a latte might be annoying, waiting for healthcare, government assistance, or even your next meal is an entirely different reality. The systems that manage our daily lives weren't built with fairness in mind, and for millions of people, time itself has become a luxury they can't afford.

Let's take a look at the DMV as a case study. Research consistently shows that wealthier neighborhoods often experience better-staffed and more efficiently run government services. In contrast, lower-income areas face longer wait times for the same tasks—renewing a license, registering a car, or applying for assistance.

For example, a 2021 study by the National Bureau of Economic Research found that low-income individuals spend an average of 12 minutes longer waiting for basic services compared to higher-income individuals. That might not sound like that big of a deal—until you realize it means you've lost six hours a month of your life just waiting for things that rich people breeze through like VIPs at a club.

If that wasn't frustrating enough, here's where things get even more infuriating: not only do the wealthy wait less, but now, they can literally buy their way to the front of the line—while everyone else just watches the gap widen.

The Rise of Pay-to-Skip Services

If you've got money, waiting becomes optional. From airport fast lanes to Disney's Lightning Lane passes, businesses have found ways to monetize impatience. Those who can afford it skip ahead, while everyone else watches the wait time grow. These systems don't merely favor wealth; they widen the gap, creating two tiers of waiting—one for the haves and another for the have-nots.

In Nigeria, waiting has become a service you can outsource—if you can afford it. 'Queue vendors' will stand in line for you at banks or fuel stations, turning time into a transaction and proving that *not* waiting is a privilege only the rich can afford.

The Emotional Cost of Inequality

Waiting longer isn't only unfair—it's maddening. Watching others pay to skip the line only rubs it in, leaving those stuck with public systems feeling disenfranchised and powerless. A single mother waiting six hours at a free health clinic while her boss texts about her absence faces a level of stress that no Disney Lightning Lane can alleviate.

Every long wait is more than wasted time—it's a symbol of a system where wealth buys convenience, and everyone else pays with hours, stress, and exhaustion.

Setting the Stage for Solutions

The good news? Change is possible. Cities like Singapore are already showing how investment in infrastructure can reduce wait times for everyone. Their AI-driven public transit system dynamically adjusts schedules to meet demand, ensuring buses and trains arrive on time regardless of neighborhood income levels.

Environmental innovations also offer promise. For instance, shared e-scooters and bike-sharing programs in cities like Copenhagen are cutting down on traffic and reducing transit wait times for all. Imagine applying these ideas globally, especially in underserved areas where the stakes are highest.

Technology can also level the playing field. Mobile scheduling apps and virtual queue systems, such as those used in Finland's government services, allow citizens to book appointments remotely, ensuring no one has to sacrifice an entire day to access basic resources. The challenge lies in ensuring these innovations are equitable—available to everyone, not simply the tech-savvy or well-off.

No One Likes a Line-Cutter

Let's be honest—no one likes a line-cutter. Cities have already cracked the code on how to make life move faster for everyone, not just those with the means to skip ahead. Smarter public transit, virtual queues, and streamlined services prove efficiency doesn't have to come at the expense of fairness. But when skipping the line becomes a privilege, something's gone terribly wrong.

And let's be real—they're already monetizing it. If we let it go unchecked, they'll just find new ways to exploit us, stretching the wait for everyone else while charging top dollar to bypass it.

At some point, we're going to have to stop grumbling and collectively say it loud enough for them to hear:

"Hey! The line starts back there."

Chapter Ten

Loading… The New Waiting, How Tech Swapped Lines for Lags

"Stuck in the middle with you. And I'm wondering what it is I should do" – Stealers Wheel,
(*You and your frozen browser tab, trapped in an unresponsive void together.*)

Ah, technology. Our savior from the agonies of waiting—or so we thought. If you've ever stared at a spinning wheel of death or cursed your Wi-Fi for buffering mid-binge, you know the truth: technology has simply swapped one kind of waiting for another. Sure, it's reduced some delays—but it's also invented entirely new ones. Welcome to the paradox of modern waiting.

We thought the future would free us from lines, delays, and wasted time. Instead, it just rebranded the wait—shuffling us from physical queues to the Wi-Fi wasteland, where the buffering wheel is just the new velvet rope. Sure, some waits have shrunk, but new ones have taken their place, and somehow, they feel even more maddening. Welcome to the paradox of modern waiting.

From Horse-and-Buggy to Hyperloop: The Evolution of Efficiency

Technology's promise has always been faster, better,

now. Ride-sharing apps whisk us away in minutes. Streaming platforms let us watch an entire season of TV without so much as rewinding. And yet, for every logistical miracle, there's a fresh irritation: the endless loop of "Your estimated delivery time is now updated to... someday."

Imagine downloads and updates, for example. A century ago, you'd be waiting for a letter to cross the Atlantic; today, you're waiting for your operating system to install version 18.3.1 (and praying it doesn't restart midway). Progress? Sure. Less frustrating? Debatable.

The Infuriating Dance of "Optimization"

Queue management systems promise to streamline lines, reduce delays, and improve customer experiences. Sometimes, though, they seem more focused on maximizing profits than on efficiency.

Airline boarding systems are the ultimate exercise in cat herding. In theory, airlines claim they board passengers in a way that minimizes congestion and speeds up the process. In reality? It often feels like a social experiment in controlled frustration.

Most airlines begin by boarding first-class and elite passengers—the chosen ones with real legroom—followed by premium economy. They then proceed with a zone-based system, often starting from the front of the plane and working backward, with Zone 1 at the front and higher-numbered zones toward the back. The logic? Supposedly, this reduces bottlenecks. The reality? It's complete chaos.

Coach passengers in later boarding groups must squeeze past those already seated, maneuvering through a gauntlet of elbows, oversized carry-ons, and aisle standstills. Overhead bins become a battlefield as people desperately shove bags into non-existent spaces, while the rest of the plane waits, glaring. It's like playing reverse Tetris—only now you've paid extra to get clocked by someone's roller bag.

Let's not forget the insult to injury "good seat" upcharge, even in coach ($27 for aisle 28 middle seat. Really?)—a stark reminder that in air travel, every inch of comfort comes with a price tag. By the time the final group is called, you're left wondering if hitchhiking might have been the better option.

By now, you'd think we'd be used to waiting—after all, we've been standing in lines and shuffling onto planes for decades. But the digital age has introduced a whole new kind of frustration: the kind where you can't even see the line you're stuck in.

The Psychology of Tech-Induced Waiting

Technology has completely changed how we wait. Standing in line for coffee might be annoying, but waiting for an online purchase to go through feels like the universe is testing your patience. Why? Digital waiting has no clues to make it bearable. There's no line, no clear sense of progress—just you, a spinning wheel, and the sinking dread that after five minutes of waiting, you hit refresh and now you're pretty sure you've been charged twice.

Even worse, tech-induced waiting often comes with false hope. The spinning wheel suggests things are moving, but are they? It's Schrödinger's progress: you're both waiting and not waiting, trapped in a paradox where time moves but nothing actually happens.

At least when you're stuck in traffic, you know exactly why you're not moving. But in the digital world, you're at the mercy of mysterious forces—server overloads, bad Wi-Fi, or some cosmic prank designed to keep you from checking out before the flash sale ends.

The Waiting Game: A Saga of Modern Frustrations

You place an order. The confirmation email arrives. The package is "out for delivery." Then it's delayed. Then it's... *somewhere*. No further details, just a vague promise that it's "on the way." You check the tracking updates obsessively, watching as your package embarks on a grand tour of regional distribution centers, bouncing between cities like it's on a soul-searching road trip.

Then there's the special kind of betrayal reserved for streaming services. You're locked in, emotionally invested, just as your show reaches its climax... and then—buffering. The screen freezes, your protagonist mid-gasp, the dreaded spinning wheel mocking you. You stare at your router, silently questioning if you've somehow offended the Wi-Fi gods. Would sacrificing a forgotten Ethernet cable to the tech spirits restore the connection? You'll never know, because at this point, you're already restarting your device, your faith in modern convenience slowly eroding.

And let's talk about virtual queues for customer support—the digital purgatory where hope goes to die. You're assured a representative will be with you "shortly," which is corporate-speak for "cancel your plans." The hold music loops on an endless, chirpy cycle, punctuated by the occasional, hollow reassurance: *Your call is important to us.* You glance at the screen. You're number 47 in line. You weigh your options: endure, hang up, or surrender to the existential dread of realizing you may never actually speak to a human being again.

At this point, you're not just waiting—you're questioning everything. Technology, capitalism, the choices that led you here. But nothing tests your patience (or your wallet) quite like when waiting isn't just inconvenient—it actually costs you money.

When Waiting Costs More Than the Purchase

Technology keeps creating new ways to make us wait, but it should also focus on making those waits less maddening—especially when major online transactions are at stake. When systems fail, they don't just waste time; they lead to failed payments, forcing customers to spend even more time resolving issues.

The impact isn't small. According to a report from Aite-Novarica Group, an estimated 117 million failed transactions occur each year, costing businesses and banks a staggering $120 billion annually. The average cost per failed transaction? Around $100—a price tag that includes customer service expenses, lost sales, and the cost of fixing system glitches. Research from The Baymard Institute also found that nearly 70% of online shopping carts are abandoned, with failed or slow payment processing being one of the biggest culprits.

These inefficiencies frustrate customers and create a ripple effect across the economy. A study by PYMNTS.com highlights that businesses experiencing frequent transaction failures see a 20% higher customer churn rate, meaning lost long-term revenue and brand trust. The irony? While technology is supposed to make transactions seamless, poor payment systems ensure that customers end up spending more time—not less—navigating digital roadblocks.

It's a costly reminder that the spinning wheel of death isn't merely mocking you—it's running up the entire system's tab.

Are Waiting Times Really Getting Worse?

It's easy to believe that waiting has reached new levels of unbearable. After all, wasn't life supposed to be faster by now? We have same-day shipping, high-speed internet, and express everything. So why does it still feel like we spend half our lives waiting for something? Are we actually waiting more, or have we just become really, really bad at dealing with any delay longer than a TikTok video?

Traffic Congestion: A Never-Ending Story

Let's start with traffic—the ultimate symbol of collective frustration.

Imagine this: your commute is 15 miles each way, and during rush hour, it takes 90 minutes round trip. Without delays, driving the speed limit should take only 45 minutes. That means you're losing 90 minutes a day—just sitting there, inching forward, staring at the same bumper sticker that stopped being funny 30 minutes ago.

Now, let's zoom out. Over a five-day workweek, that's 7.5 hours wasted in traffic. In a year? Nearly 400 hours gone. And over a 50-year career, a single commuter could spend 20,000 hours—more than two full years of their life—stuck in gridlock.

And it's not only you. Multiply that by the millions of other bleary-eyed, coffee-fueled commuters—let's call them the Fellowship of the Miserably Stuck—and suddenly, society is bleeding away entire lifetimes to traffic.

And for what? So some out-of-touch exec can force people back to the office five days a week to "collaborate" over Zoom with the rest of their team...who are working remotely from other locations. If traffic congestion is a crisis, the five-day in-office mandate is the villain twirling its mustache.

And that's just for work. Add in all the extra time wasted running errands, getting to appointments, or trying to make a "quick" trip across town, and the numbers get even uglier.

Traffic is more than an inconvenience—it's a time thief of epic proportions.

Customer Service: The Hold Line From Hell

Customer service hold times are another familiar gripe. Over the past decade, average wait times for call centers have fluctuated depending on the industry. For instance:

Tech support: 17 minutes on average.

Healthcare providers: 29 minutes on average.

Airlines during holiday seasons: "Indefinite"—or so it feels.

Your Call Is Very Important to Us… Please Hold for Eternity

According to a Talkdesk Research Report, Americans spend an average of 13 hours annually waiting on hold for customer service. Over an 82-year lifetime, that adds up to a staggering 1,066 hours, or about 44 days, listening to hold music.

It's not just an American problem. In the UK, Britons collectively spend an astonishing 800 years annually waiting to speak to HM Revenue & Customs, according to a study by Which? It makes the Beatles' *Taxman* feel oddly prophetic—except now they'd need to add a verse about endless hold music. Collectively, these waits aren't just frustrating; they're a colossal waste of time that could be better spent on literally anything else.

The Pandemic's Impact on Waiting

The COVID-19 pandemic took waiting to absurd new heights. Supply chain chaos left shipping containers stuck at ports, turning two-day delivery into a six-week saga. According to a report from UNCTAD (United Nations Conference on Trade and Development), global maritime trade shrank by 7.0% to 9.6% during the first eight months of 2020, leading to an estimated $412 billion in economic losses. The backlog at major ports like Los Angeles and Shanghai caused ripple effects across industries, showing just how fragile just-in-time supply chains could be. If you think waiting on hold for customer service is bad, at least you weren't stuck *physically* waiting in a 60-mile gridlock for nearly two weeks.

Medical systems were similarly overwhelmed. A Kaiser Family Foundation survey found that 41% of U.S. adults delayed or skipped medical care due to the pandemic, as hospitals struggled to keep up with surging cases. Non-urgent appointments became as rare as Bigfoot sightings, exposing deep vulnerabilities in healthcare systems worldwide.

While the pandemic showed us how fragile global logistics could be, there's one wait that stands in a category of its own—a legendary traffic jam so absurd, so mind-bogglingly slow, it deserves its own chapter in the history of human endurance.

The 60-Mile Jam That Became Its Own City

Imagine this: you're cruising along the Beijing-Tibet Expressway in August 2010, maybe humming a tune or mentally drafting your resignation email. Suddenly, the traffic slows. Then it stops. And then... it *really* stops. What started as an ordinary delay morphed into the most infamous traffic jam in modern history—a sprawling 60-mile snarl that held drivers hostage for up to 12 days. Yes, days. Not hours. Not "hey, let's take a nap in the car." Days.

The culprit? A trifecta of bad luck, bad planning, and a dash of chaos. Construction on the highway had reduced lanes, creating bottlenecks. To make matters worse, an spike of trucks carrying coal from Inner Mongolia overloaded the system. Throw in a few breakdowns, and bingo—a highway transformed into a parking lot that stretched longer than some small countries.

By day two, it became clear: this wasn't just a traffic jam; it was *life now*. Cars and trucks weren't just vehicles anymore—they were homes, pop-up shops, and, for a few brave souls, personal karaoke lounges. Drivers, realizing they might be in it for the long haul, began rationing food, water, and gas. Strangers became neighbors. Truckers struck up conversations about life, coal, and how they might never see their families again.

By day five, entrepreneurial locals smelled opportunity—and profit. Vendors on bicycles appeared, selling everything from instant noodles to cigarettes, priced with the kind of markup that would make a Wall Street trader blush. Water bottles that once cost a few yuan suddenly carried luxury-item price tags. But hey, when you're dehydrated in a traffic jam with no end in sight, who's going to haggle?

As the days dragged on, the jam took on a life of its own. Groups of commuters formed micro-communities based on proximity, shared snacks, and mutual misery. Someone inevitably floated the idea of electing a mayor to organize resources (and presumably negotiate with the noodle cartel). Arguments broke out over who had the best playlist or whose truck's air conditioning was most deserving of a communal nap. The rumor mill churned faster than any car engine on that highway, with whispers of phantom lanes opening up or secret noodle discounts.

Humans are nothing if not resourceful. Drivers held impromptu cooking lessons using gas stoves perched on truck beds. Card games became the main form of entertainment, with high-stakes rounds involving the last can of soda as the ultimate prize. Some even reportedly bartered goods—"I'll trade you this half-eaten granola bar for two sips of water and your eternal friendship."

After 12 grueling days, traffic finally began to clear, though the memories lingered far longer than the fumes. The jam became a cautionary tale for urban planners and a source of dark humor for anyone stuck in their daily commute. To this day, it remains a legend—proof that, when faced with absurdity, humans adapt, innovate, and occasionally elect imaginary mayors.

So next time you're stuck in traffic, just remember: at least you're not negotiating for overpriced noodles in the world's slowest-moving city.

So, Is It Worse?

The answer is: it depends. In many ways, waiting times have improved thanks to technology and better logistics. But in other areas—like public services, healthcare, and customer support—delays have remained stubbornly long. And even when waits are shorter, our heightened expectations make them feel unbearable.

Part IV

Innovations and Solutions

Chapter Eleven

Part I

Delays for Days: Industries That Keep You in a Waiting Haze

"Hello... is it me you're looking for?" – Lionel Richie, *Hello* (*Yes, customer service—it is. If you could pick up before I age another decade, that'd be great.*)

Waiting is an equal-opportunity menace—it doesn't care who you are, where you live, or how important you think you are. It slithers into every industry, from transportation to healthcare to customer service, grinding progress to a halt and ensuring that millions of people spend their precious time screaming at automated phone systems or contemplating the mysteries of life in a checkout line. If inefficiency were an Olympic sport, some industries would be perennial gold medalists.

Consider transportation, The Texas A&M Transportation Institute reports that the average driver in Los Angeles loses 119 hours per year to congestion—basically an unpaid part-time job. That's roughly three full workweeks a year lost to staring at taillights, listening to the same five songs on repeat, and contemplating whether you should just abandon your car and start a new life on foot. Then there's customer service, an industry that has mastered the art of making you suffer in a queue, both physical and digital. The average American spends 43 days of their life on hold—that's more than a month of listening to smooth jazz and robotic assurances that "your call is very important to us."

Few experiences are as universally dreaded as waiting in a medical setting where waiting has been elevated to an endurance sport. Need an appointment with a specialist? That'll be several weeks in the U.S., assuming you're lucky. Over in the ER, they've perfected the art of making you reconsider how "urgent" your broken arm actually is.

Across industries, waiting is more than a minor inconvenience—it's a multi-billion-dollar disaster. From supply chain failures that leave store shelves barren to bureaucratic bottlenecks that turn paperwork into a time loop, businesses are bleeding money while consumers are bleeding patience. The worst part? We've somehow come to accept this as normal.

Before we get to the solutions, let's take a good, hard look at just how bad the problem really is. Saddle up, tater tot—it's about to get frustrating.

Healthcare: Take a Number, Take a Nap

Healthcare delays are where even the most patient among us start considering if medieval barbers really had the right idea with the whole 'just cut it off' approach.

Hurry Up and Wait: The Specialist Edition

Need to see a specialist? Hope you're patient—literally. The average wait time for a medical specialist in the U.S. is about a month, but depending on what ails you, it could be even worse. Neurology? About 5 weeks. Dermatology? A solid month (hope that rash isn't in a hurry). Psychiatry? 6 to 7 weeks—and that's just to *talk* about your stress, not fix it. In some areas, wait times for certain specialists stretch into months, which is a fun little paradox when you need an orthopedic surgeon because you broke your leg yesterday.

Some of the biggest delays come from a shortage of doctors, rising patient demand, and an appointment system that often feels like it was designed by an evil mastermind. Studies have shown that specialist wait times vary widely by region, with some cities averaging over 50 days for appointments, while in smaller towns, you might get in within a couple of weeks—assuming you don't mind driving 200 miles to get there.

While AI-powered scheduling tools and telemedicine are helping reduce the wait in some cases, they can't magically create more doctors or make hospitals suddenly efficient. So for now, the real trick to getting faster care? Book your appointment ahead of time—say, a few years before you actually get sick.

Surgery Delays: Plenty of Time to Say Goodbye to Your Original Knees

So, you need a non-urgent medical procedure in the U.S.? Brace yourself, because the wait might be long enough for you to develop a deep, personal connection with your pain. Knee replacement? Four to six months—plenty of time to pick out a stylish cane and name it something cool. Cataract surgery? One to three months—more than enough time to pretend your smudged glasses are the real problem. Hernia repair? Somewhere between "soon" and "have you considered just living with it?"

And this isn't only a U.S. problem. Canadians can wait over a year for some elective surgeries, which makes free healthcare feel like an elaborate patience test. The UK's NHS aims for 18-week wait times, but reality often laughs at those goals. Meanwhile, in Germany and Switzerland, wait times are so short they'd be considered a medical miracle elsewhere, weeks instead of months. Turns out, efficiency applies to more than just their train systems.

Naturally, while you're waiting, your condition might get worse, forcing a routine procedure to become an emergency one. But hey, at least that moves you to the front of the line! Nothing like gaming the system with a full-blown health crisis. So if you're looking to schedule surgery, go ahead and make that appointment preemptively—maybe for an ailment you don't even have yet, just to get a head start.

Government Agencies: Where Time Goes to Die

The DMV, immigration offices, and city planning departments exist in a separate time zone known as Eventual Standard Time (EST), where everything takes longer than you think—and then even longer than that. But again, it's not always the wait that's unbearable—it's the feeling of being stuck in limbo with no clue when it will end.

And let's not forget the fine art of government paperwork, where no form is ever the right form, and every completed document spawns three new ones you didn't know you needed. You stand in line for two hours, finally reach the counter, and—surprise!—you forgot Form 27B/6, the one that requires a notarized signature from your childhood dentist and a blood oath to the bureaucracy gods. Back to the end of the line you go.

Of course, some government agencies have tried to modernize, moving services online to reduce wait times. The result? You now get to experience the same frustration remotely, as you repeatedly refresh a glitchy website that crashes the moment you finally upload the right document. Progress!

And just when you think you've made it through, they drop the final boss battle: the "We'll process this in 6-8 weeks" message. Six to eight weeks? For what? Are they chiseling the documents onto stone tablets? Growing the paper from sustainably sourced trees in the agency's backyard? No one knows. All you can do is wait.

Trial by Jury? More Like Trial by Calendar

Justice delayed is justice denied—but let's be real, courts have never been known for speed. A simple traffic ticket can take months to resolve, while high-stakes criminal trials can stretch on for years. According to the U.S. Bureau of Justice Statistics, the median time for felony cases to reach a resolution in state courts is over 256 days—and that's just the average. In civil courts, things move even slower, with backlogged dockets pushing some trials out by two to three years before they even get a court date. Overcrowded dockets and understaffed courts mean that even the most straightforward cases take so long, people start to forget what they were arguing about in the first place.

And heaven help you if you're dealing with a bureaucratic nightmare like a property dispute or a probate case—those can stretch on so long that by the time a verdict is reached, the original parties might not even be around to hear it. (Nothing like your grandkids finally inheriting that landlocked parcel of swamp you spent a decade fighting over.) Meanwhile, some criminal cases drag on so long that the defendants could've used the time to go to law school themselves and represent their own appeal.

And if you're one of the lucky souls summoned for jury duty, congrats—you've just won an unpaid, all-inclusive vacation to a government building where the coffee tastes like burnt battery acid, the chairs are designed for maximum discomfort, and the only entertainment is watching a lawyer perform the legal equivalent of interpretive dance, stalling for three hours over an objection so convoluted that even the judge is Googling 'how to fake your own death' mid-trial.

Traffic: The Modern Sisyphus

As we previously pointed out, If you drive 30 minutes to and from work daily, you spend 125 hours a year just waiting. Nationwide, TTI estimates that congestion costs the U.S. economy $87 billion annually in lost productivity and wasted fuel.

Now, if you're thinking, *well, that's just how modern life works*, I will soon introduce you to the cities that have decided gridlock isn't a law of nature, but a problem with a very fixable solution. Because while we're sitting bumper to bumper, screaming at Waze for rerouting us onto an even worse street, other places have actually figured out how to keep things moving.

I'd Like to Speak to a Human: A Tragic Saga

Waiting on hold used to be an exercise in patience—now it's an exercise in finding new ways to scream "REPRESENTATIVE!" into your phone. Customer service has always been the front line in the war on waiting—a never-ending battle of hold music, vague promises, and "your call is very important to us." For decades, companies have been throwing every technology and strategy they can think of at it, trying to minimize hold times and smooth out support processes—with results that range from "almost helpful" to "please scream into the void."

Now, instead of sitting on hold listening to smooth jazz, we're now pressing 1 for this, 2 for that, yelling that before mentioned "REPRESENTATIVE" into the phone, and navigating chatbots that act like they've never heard of your problem before. It's like customer service looked at hold music and thought, "What if we made it interactive—and somehow worse?"

At this point, customer service isn't solving problems—it's a gladiator-style endurance test to see how long you can tolerate nonsense before giving up entirely. But here's the real question: Have we just accepted all of this as the cost of modern life? Or is there actually a way to beat the system? Let's find out.

Chapter Eleven

Part II

The Battle Plan – How We're Fighting the Wait

"Is this the real life? Is this just fantasy?"
– Queen, *Bohemian Rhapsody*
(*Spoken aloud while watching a deepfake of yourself singing this very song.*)

Now that we've sufficiently complained about waiting, let's get to the good stuff: the solutions. AI, automation, and some good old-fashioned human ingenuity are making waits shorter, smarter, and occasionally even enjoyable.

Paging Doctor Patience

Healthcare might be one of the few arenas where waiting feels uniquely personal—and universally frustrating. Whether it's the interminable black hole of boredom of a waiting room or the weeks-long agony of scheduling an appointment, the system often feels designed to test our patience. But recent innovations are reshaping how we experience healthcare, making the process faster, more efficient, and dare we say—less miserable.

AI in Healthcare: Goodbye Waiting Rooms

Let's start with one of humanity's most dreaded waiting experiences: the waiting room. AI is being used to shake things up by streamlining everything from appointment scheduling to triage. Tools like Babylon Health and Ada Health use AI to assess symptoms, prioritize care, and even suggest treatments—all before you've set foot in a clinic.

Instead of waiting six weeks to see a specialist only to be told, "Whoops, you actually need a different specialist—see you in another six weeks," AI systems are finally stepping in to save patients from this medical version of a wild goose chase.

For example, Mayo Clinic's AI-powered referral system, uses machine learning and natural language processing to analyze a patient's symptoms, medical history, and diagnostic data to recommend the right specialist the first time, instead of just blindly setting you up with the first available doctor.

Then there's eConsult, an AI-driven platform that lets general practitioners electronically consult specialists before even sending the patient in. This has cut unnecessary referrals by up to 70%, which means fewer people are sitting in a waiting room for two hours only to be told, "Yeah, this isn't my department." The UK's NHS has widely adopted it, making it one of the few examples of bureaucracy actually working in someone's favor.

While Dr. Google continues sending people into full-blown panic, telemedicine platforms like K Health and Buoy Health have developed AI-powered chatbots that triage your symptoms and match you with the right type of doctor before you even book an appointment. So instead of wasting a month waiting for a neurologist to tell you that, no, it's just heartburn, AI steps in and says, "Hey, buddy, maybe see a gastroenterologist instead."

Even Cleveland Clinic has hopped on the AI express (though, let's be real, they were probably driving the thing before the rest of us even found the station). They've rolled out an AI triage tool that analyzes medical records, symptom severity, and risk factors to make sure you don't spend weeks waiting for an orthopedic specialist when you really need a neurologist. A study in The Lancet Digital Health found that AI triage tools correctly identify urgent cases 90% of the time, compared to 75% for traditional triage nurses—which is great news for anyone who'd rather not play medical roulette with their referrals. Because as much as a sore knee is annoying, it's not exactly causing those dizzy spells.

These AI-driven systems are already proving that technology can cut out the unnecessary waiting, reduce frustration, and make sure people actually get the medical help they need—before they've aged out of their insurance plan.

In hospitals, AI manages operating room schedules, juggling emergency surgeries and routine procedures like a virtuoso conductor leading a particularly chaotic orchestra. And for those of us who dread waiting on hold with healthcare providers, AI-powered chatbots are stepping in, answering basic questions, booking appointments, and even following up after visits. Sure, they're not perfect, but they're better than the alternative: spending 45 minutes listening to hold music and wondering if the receptionist just forgot about you.

Denmark's Bispebjerg Hospital in Copenhagen is leading the charge in AI-powered surgery scheduling. Their machine learning system crunches patient data, predicts peak demand, and adjusts schedules in real time to keep things running smoothly. The result? More patients treated faster, fewer operating rooms left on standby instead of in service, and wait times for non-urgent surgeries slashed from months to just a few weeks.

Best of all, it's put an end to the high-stakes game of operating room musical chairs. Instead, everything runs with the precision of a Michelin-starred kitchen—minus the yelling. And perhaps most impressively, it's managed to cut wait times without the usual side effect of hospital lobbies turning into chaotic mobs demanding faster service.

AI Summaries: Turning Chaos into Clarity

Let's face it: doctor's visits can be a blur—you're nodding along, eyes glazing over, trying to absorb a flood of medical jargon while also low-key panicking about whether you should have WebMD'd your symptoms first (reminder to self: *you shouldn't*). As your doctor multitasks like a caffeinated octopus, they're simultaneously juggling you, their notes, and a never-ending cascade of paperwork, all while the clock keeps ticking toward their next patient. It's a high-speed exchange where you leave in a daze wondering what the hell just happened.

Then there's the waiting—for the follow-up appointment, for test results, for the moment you finally remember what the doctor actually said. Was it "exercise more" or "extra s'mores?" Hard to say, but one sounds significantly more appealing. Luckily, AI is stepping in to make sense of it all, ensuring you spend less time guessing and more time actually following the right advice.

Systems like Suki AI, Nuance DAX (Dragon Ambient eXperience), and Abridge are transforming doctor-patient interactions by automatically transcribing and summarizing conversations in real time. These AI-powered assistants extract key medical insights, generate structured notes, and integrate them into electronic health records (EHRs), cutting documentation time by up to 50%. That means doctors spend less time typing and more time actually listening to patients—which is a win for everyone involved.

Even better, these AI-generated summaries aren't just for doctors—they're also becoming accessible to patients via platforms like MyChart and other patient portals. So instead of waiting days for a follow-up call or relying on your half-remembered mental notes, you can log in, review your visit summary, check prescribed treatments, and follow up on next steps—all without playing a guessing game.

In other words, AI isn't only helping doctors save time—it's giving patients more control over theirs. Because while waiting will always be a part of life, it doesn't have to be as much of a part of your healthcare experience. And if technology can make doctor's visits clearer, faster, and less stressful? Well, that's a wait *actually* worth eliminating.

Telemedicine: Bringing the Doctor to You

No more slogging your way through traffic, sitting in a germ-infested waiting room thumbing through a grimy 1974 copy of Reader's Digest with a cougher behind you. Thanks to telemedicine, you can now consult a doctor from your couch, armed with nothing but a Wi-Fi connection and a vague sense of concern over that weird rash.

And people are embracing it in record numbers. In 2020 alone, telemedicine usage skyrocketed by 154%, according to the CDC, as people rightfully decided that visiting a doctor in person during a pandemic wasn't ideal. The trend hasn't slowed down—by 2023, 37% of adults in the U.S. had used telemedicine in the past year, a massive leap from just 7% in 2019. The global telemedicine market, valued at $87.2 billion in 2022, is expected to surpass $455 billion by 2030, proving that virtual doctor visits aren't just a pandemic-era fad—they're here to stay.

Platforms like Teladoc, Amwell, and MDLIVE now cover everything from urgent care to mental health therapy, making healthcare more accessible than ever. A study by McKinsey found that 76% of patients prefer telemedicine for routine check-ups and minor ailments because it saves time, eliminates unnecessary in-person visits, and lets them receive care in their pajamas—which, frankly, should have been a healthcare goal all along.

Yet, quirks remain. Diagnosing a rash over grainy webcam footage can feel like a medical guessing game, and spotty Wi-Fi can turn a critical diagnosis into a game of charades. Some doctors worry about the limitations of virtual exams, and not all insurance plans fully cover telemedicine visits, making accessibility still somewhat uneven.

Despite these hiccups, telemedicine is revolutionizing healthcare, cutting down wait times, increasing access for rural patients, and even reducing ER visits by 15% as more people turn to virtual consultations instead of unnecessary emergency room trips. With AI-powered diagnostics and more advanced remote monitoring tools on the horizon, telemedicine is proving that, in many cases, the doctor really can come to you—no waiting room required.

Bureaucracy: AI vs. the Red Tape Hydra

Few things in life are as patience-draining as waiting for government paperwork. Need a permit? That'll be six to eight weeks. Want a passport renewal? Hope you brought snacks.

AI is here to turn this paper-pushing purgatory into something almost bearable. Governments worldwide are adopting AI to streamline processes, from renewing driver's licenses to filing taxes. Chatbots like Australia's "Alex" or Singapore's "Ask Jamie" help citizens navigate confusing forms and answer questions in seconds. AI even helps identify errors or missing information before you submit, saving you from the dreaded "we regret to inform you" letter months later.

Immigration services are also benefiting from AI's efficiency. Algorithms now analyze and process visa applications faster than ever, flagging inconsistencies or high-risk profiles without holding up everyone else's paperwork. While it's not perfect—AI still struggles with nuance and context—it's a step up from waiting six months to find out you checked the wrong box.

Now Serving... Yourself: Kiosks Take Over Bureaucracy

In places like New York City and Hamburg, bureaucracy has had a digital glow-up where they've introduced self-service kiosks to streamline government processes. In New York, the DMV allows residents to renew driver's licenses and vehicle registrations without ever speaking to a human (or realizing they've aged three years while waiting for their number to be called). Hamburg has taken it a step further with digital self-service stations where citizens can apply for passports, ID cards, and residence permits—reminding the rest of us that government efficiency doesn't have to be a mythical creature, whispered about but never seen.

Singapore vs. Slow Justice: Case Closed

While some legal systems seem committed to the fine art of delay, Singapore took a different approach—one that doesn't involve waiting so long that the original dispute becomes ancient history. Enter the Community Justice and Tribunals System (CJTS), an AI-powered online platform that lets users file claims, submit evidence, and even attend virtual hearings without setting foot in a courtroom. No more scheduling nightmares, no more stacks of paperwork—it's as close to 'one-click justice' as modern bureaucracy allows.

And for cases that still require court time, the Intelligent Case Management System (ICMS) takes over, automating scheduling, prioritizing urgent cases, and flagging administrative bottlenecks before they become full-blown backlogs. The result? Faster trial times, fewer case backlogs, and a system that actually respects the concept of 'justice in a timely manner'. It's almost like they think the law should actually work for people. Wild concept.

DMVs: Now With 30% Less Suffering

The days of taking a number, clutching it like a lifeline, and settling in for hours of afternoon-ruining plastic chair time might finally be on their way out—at least in the more forward-thinking corners of the DMV universe. Many DMVs are ditching the old "sit and suffer" model for shiny new online appointment systems, where you can book a specific time slot in advance, skip the chaos, and almost feel like the DMV respects your time. Almost. This simple upgrade keeps crowds under control and helps staff manage workflows without looking like deer in headlights.

If you're the spontaneous type who loves to roll the dice and show up unannounced, real-time queue apps are here to save you from your own adventurous spirit. States like Kansas, Indiana, and Idaho lead the charge with digital queue systems that let you check wait times before leaving the house. Whether you're joining a virtual line via the QLess system in Kansas, taking advantage of Indiana's digital updates that have slashed average waits from 40 minutes to just 8, or breezing through Idaho's efficient scheduling tools, these apps are making DMV visits far less painful. They spare you the heartbreak of discovering a three-hour line when all you've packed is a single granola bar, a 20% charged phone, and a vague sense of regret.

And that's just the start. In several states, self-service kiosks are stepping in to handle routine tasks like license renewals or vehicle registrations. Think of them as ATMs for bureaucratic misery—quick, efficient, and blissfully free of awkward small talk with stressed-out clerks. For instance, South Carolina's DMV Express kiosks allow residents to renew vehicle registrations in less than two minutes, providing a fast and easy alternative to traditional office visits.

As the DMV slowly enters the 21st century, mobile apps are making DMV visits practically optional, letting you handle scheduling, notifications, and even payments from the comfort of your couch (and sweatpants). States like Louisiana have introduced digital driver's licenses through apps like LA Wallet, enabling residents to access their ID digitally and renew their physical license or ID through the app.

No revolution is without its hiccups. Some DMVs are still working with systems that look like they were installed when floppy disks were cutting-edge. And while automation is great, there's no AI smart enough yet to explain why your number hasn't been called after an hour when the screen says "Now Serving: No One." But with enough investment in staff and infrastructure, maybe one day the DMV will be more like a pit stop and less like a government-sponsored escape room. Until then, at least you've got an app for that.

Immigration and Legal Processes: Streamlining the Red Tape

Nothing pushes the limits of human endurance quite like immigration and legal paperwork, but automation is stepping in to untangle the red tape (to save you at least a few hours). Governments are embracing AI to process forms and applications faster, from visa approvals to tax refunds—less waiting, fewer headaches. Australia's automated border systems, for instance, have turned customs queues into a quick pit stop, freeing travelers to enjoy the Outback instead of glaring at customs officers.

Still, it's not all smooth sailing. Backlogs remain a stubborn problem in many countries, thanks to a mix of outdated systems that probably predate the Internet and funding levels that scream "do more with less... again." Even the flashiest tech can hit a wall when overwhelmed by demand, proving that while AI is great at crunching data, it can't replace the basics—like enough staff and resources to keep the wheels turning. After all, even the best-designed system can't outrun a fax machine that refuses to die.

Global Examples: Leading the Way

Estonia, often dubbed the "most digital country in the world," has embraced e-governance to an extraordinary degree. Citizens can perform nearly every government transaction online, from voting to filing taxes, often in just a matter of minutes. The result is virtually no waiting in government offices.

Singapore's efficiency obsession extends to its passport processing, where biometric tech like facial and iris recognition means your face does all the paperwork. With most applications done in hours, it makes other countries' systems look positively medieval by comparison.

Challenges and Backlogs: Not Quite Perfect Yet

Not even the best systems are immune to roadblocks. Backlogs persist globally, often due to tech that's older than disco and funding that's more theoretical than practical. In the U.S., your DMV experience might range from high-tech efficiency to a historical reenactment of 1970s bureaucracy. Some states have streamlined processes with automation, while others are still fumbling through system crashes like a toddler with an iPad. And while automation can work wonders when it's actually working, it's far from foolproof—glitches have left millions of applications mysteriously "stuck in the system," delayed for months, or riddled with errors.

California's DMV upgrade in 2018 famously botched over a million voter registrations due to system malfunctions, proving that even well-intentioned modernization can go spectacularly wrong. And California isn't alone—across the country, attempts to digitize the DMV have resulted in everything from months-long delays for driver's licenses to online renewal systems that randomly double-charge users or refuse to process payments altogether, turning expired licenses into an unintentional lifestyle choice. In some places, the mess has been so bad that people have resorted to camping out overnight just to get service—because nothing says *"the future is here"* like sleeping in a folding chair outside a government building.

Then there's the human factor: no algorithm can prevent the occasional employee from going "on break" just as a line stretches out the door.

Still, progress is undeniable. Governments may not move at startup speed, but their push to modernize public services is finally paying off. Online appointments, automated forms, and queue-tracking apps turn bureaucratic waiting from a marathon into a light jog. And the financial savings are just as compelling—Estonia, for example, saves 2% of its GDP through digitization, while U.S. states are saving millions by streamlining processes.

If Singapore and Estonia can turn waiting into a thing of the past, there's no reason the rest of the world can't follow suit. It might take some time, but with digital passports, automated forms, and queue apps paving the way, the days of endless waiting could soon be over—one streamlined system at a time.

The Great Transportation Upgrade: Beating Traffic, Delays, and Shipping Chaos

Traffic is the OG waiting game, and for decades, the only real strategy was honking aggressively and muttering under your breath. But today, we're seeing a new wave of tech-driven solutions that are transforming not only how we drive, but how everything moves—from people to packages to supply chains.

Supply Chains: Smarter Routes, Faster Deliveries

Waiting affects more than just people—it can trigger multi-trillion-dollar supply chain disasters. Every year, logistics bottlenecks, shipping delays, and inefficient transport systems cost the global economy an estimated $1.6 trillion (yes, with a T) in lost productivity and added expenses.

According to a study by the World Economic Forum, inefficiencies in transportation and logistics inflate costs by up to 15% of global GDP—which is basically like setting piles of money on fire and then waiting three weeks for more kindling to arrive.

Captain Jacked Sparrow and the $60 Billion Oops

The Suez Canal Incident: Brought to You by the Letter 'F'

Annoyed by your two-day shipping delay? Cute. Imagine a quarter of the world's shipping traffic grinding to a halt because one ship decided to do the world's worst parallel park and t-boned the Suez Canal. In 2021, the Ever Given, a container ship roughly the size of the Empire State Building, somehow managed to wedge itself completely sideways in the canal, blocking 12% of global trade for six days.

That single maritime fail racked up an estimated $60 billion in trade losses, delayed millions of shipments, and proved that, yes, one bad turn can literally ruin the global economy. Dude, you had one job, WTF. Imagine being the poor guy driving that thing, somewhere out there, his friends are probably still roasting him on their group chat. He's never gonna live that one down. Could you imagine the conversation with his wife when he got home that day? 'How was your day, honey?' 'Oh, you know, just lightly *threw a wrench in the global economy*—what's for dinner?'.

The Great Supply Chain Meltdown: When the World's Stuff Got Stuck at Sea

Turns out, bottlenecks don't just happen in canals—sometimes, they happen at the very last stop. This one started like every good disaster—slowly, then all at once.

First, a pandemic shut down factories and ports, sending shipping schedules into a tailspin. Then, people—stuck at home, armed with stimulus checks and a borderline unhealthy relationship with Amazon Prime—began ordering everything that wasn't nailed down. Demand skyrocketed, warehouses filled up, and before long, the supply chain collapsed like an overworked Jenga tower. The result? The Port of Los Angeles became the world's most exclusive parking lot, with over 100 cargo ships bobbing offshore like giant, stranded bathtub toys.

If you looked out over the California coast in late 2021, you'd have seen what can only be described as the world's saddest boat parade. Ships loaded with Christmas presents, furniture, electronics, and more toilet paper than a doomsday bunker were stuck in a traffic jam so massive that some crew members had time to grow full beards *twice* before docking. It was less of a supply chain and more of a supply clog—a logistical colon blockage that no amount of fiber could fix.

Meanwhile, on land, retailers panicked. The backlog cost them over $223 billion in lost sales, which means somewhere, a group of executives in very expensive suits sat in a boardroom weeping over graphs. Shoppers who had pre-ordered items months in advance were left wondering if they'd get their packages before their hair turned gray. By the time some goods finally arrived, they were either wildly out of season (*a winter coat in July, how thoughtful!*) or completely obsolete (*enjoy your brand-new 2021 Smart TV, now featuring last year's technology!*).

To make matters worse, all those idling ships weren't just bad for business—they were *terrible* for the air. With nowhere to go, these floating diesel-belching behemoths transformed Los Angeles into a real-life *Mad Max* set, pumping out enough pollution to make a rush-hour freeway feel like a crisp mountain retreat. Turns out, if you park over 100 giant cargo ships offshore for months on end, you don't just get supply chain delays—you get your very own floating smog factory.

In 2021, emissions at the Port of L.A. skyrocketed like the Exxon Valdez spill—but in the sky, with sulfur oxides (SOx) spiking 145%. That's right—SOx pollution nearly *tripled*, giving the air around the port a fine bouquet of Eau de Cargo Ship. But hey, silver lining: if you ever wanted to know what breathing inside a coal mine feels like, you didn't even have to leave the beach.

The Port of L.A. has ambitious goals to make all cargo-handling equipment zero-emissions by 2030 and all drayage trucks emissions-free by 2035. Which is great! Except... maybe they should start with making sure ships don't have to loiter offshore, belching fumes into the air like 100 chain-smoking Godzillas. It's like declaring a new diet while simultaneously ordering a double bacon cheeseburger.

And so, the Great Supply Chain Meltdown of 2021-2022 entered the history books—a cautionary tale about what happens when global logistics meets human impatience. The takeaway? If you ever wondered what life would be like if shipping containers had their own glorified floating VIP waiting lounge—well, *we all found out together*.

The World Is on Backorder

The supply chain didn't just buckle under pressure—it went down like a Jenga tower in an earthquake. And even now, with the floating ship parade mostly cleared up, we're still playing an endless game of logistical whack-a-mole. Trucks are waiting for better routes, warehouses are waiting for inventory, and somewhere right now, your online order is stranded in a facility three states away, held hostage by reasons no one can quite explain.

At some point in 2024, humans collectively took a mental health day, double-fisted a pint of beer and a venti dark roast, and decided to let AI take the wheel—because, let's be honest, solving the world's problems is exhausting, and delegation is the backbone of capitalism. So now, stepping up to the podium as our latest contestant in "Let's Fix This Mess"—Artificial Intelligence! Because why let humans screw up supply chains when we can outsource the chaos to an algorithm with the emotional range of a toaster?

But this isn't the first time someone looked at a logistical nightmare and thought, *there has to be a better way.* Back in the 1700s, Swiss mathematician Leonhard Euler tried to solve a puzzle about crossing Königsberg's seven bridges exactly once without retracing your steps. He did the math, came to a very scientific conclusion, and essentially said, *Nope. Impossible.* Euler had no idea, but he had just laid the groundwork for graph theory, the mathematical backbone of modern logistics.

Euler proved some paths just don't work—but AI, armed with ungodly processing power, refuses to accept that. It takes Euler's graph theory, smashes it against real-time data, and brute-forces solutions anyway. Your package, once at the mercy of human error and bad infrastructure, now moves through a system optimized by machines that—while completely lacking human empathy—are very good at making sure your impulse buy actually arrives before you forget why you ordered it.

And the results? Staggering. AI-driven logistics improvements are slashing delivery times and cutting billions in waste. UPS, for example, crunched the numbers and realized something weirdly simple: if their drivers avoided making left turns, they'd save a ton of money. Why? Because left turns mean idling, waiting for oncoming traffic, and burning unnecessary fuel. So they programmed their AI-powered ORION system (On-Road Integrated Optimization and Navigation) to design routes that prioritize right turns whenever possible. The result? A yearly savings of 10 million gallons of fuel and over $400 million—all because some algorithm had the good sense to tell drivers, *Hey, maybe don't sit at that intersection for five minutes trying to turn left.*

AI-powered route optimization across industries is shaving up to 30% off delivery times and increasing shipping efficiency by 65%. Global supply chain AI is projected to save companies over $1.3 trillion annually by 2035, all by squeezing inefficiencies out of a system that, until recently, relied heavily on gut instinct, spreadsheets, and truckers who "just know a better way."

And it's not just trucks—AI is rerouting cargo ships in real-time to dodge port backlogs, reorganizing warehouses so high-demand items are closer to loading docks, and deciding whether your city's stoplights should actually let traffic flow or just continue their long-standing tradition of ruining everyone's day. Companies like Convoy, Uber Freight, and Loadsmart are using AI to dynamically reroute shipments, avoid empty miles, and match drivers with loads more efficiently than autocorrect matches you with the word you actually meant to type.

Over in the world of disturbingly efficient capitalism, Amazon's fulfillment centers are so scarily good at predicting demand that they sometimes ship products to warehouses near you before you even realize you need them. This is equal parts impressive and slightly creepy, as if your shopping cart is now sentient and finishing your sentences before you even type them.

So next time your package actually arrives on time, just know that some AI system somewhere crunched millions of data points, optimized every possible route, and single-handedly prevented your order from taking an unnecessary scenic detour through Ohio. Euler walked so AI could run… and so your same-day delivery could actually be *same day*.

Public Transit That Actually Works? It's Possible.

Instead of standing on a street corner like an abandoned extra in a post-apocalyptic film, wondering if your bus will ever arrive, cities are finally embracing real-time tracking—a long-overdue upgrade to public transit that's saving time, money, and sanity.

For years, waiting for the bus has long operated on a time-honored system of "good luck, hope a bus shows up." A 2022 study by Moovit found that the average commuter in major U.S. cities spends 40 minutes per day waiting for public transit—that's 173 hours a year, or roughly an entire week every year just standing around, contemplating your life choices—starting with why you didn't just walk. Worse, 25% of bus riders reported that their buses either showed up unpredictably or not at all (*which, frankly, feels like a metaphor for modern existence*).

Finally, artificial intelligence is muscling its way into the conversation to replace outdated scheduling guesswork with real-time logic, ensuring transit systems adjust to the real-world instead of sticking to a timetable like it's written in stone. These systems help commuters and they also save cities a fortune, which means fewer budget meetings feel like a hostage negotiation over pothole repairs. According to McKinsey & Company, integrating real-time transit technology can reduce operational costs by up to 15% by optimizing bus routes, reducing idle times, and cutting down on unnecessary fuel consumption. In other words, not only does real-time tracking mean fewer missed buses, but it also means cities can stop hemorrhaging money on inefficient transit systems.

Cities like New York, London, and Singapore have rolled out tracking systems to give passengers accurate arrival times, route updates, and even alternate travel suggestions when buses are running late. London's iBus system, for example, uses GPS data and AI-powered predictions to improve bus arrival accuracy, making wait times shorter and more consistent *(which, for Londoners, is about as exciting as finding an empty Tube seat at rush hour.)*

In Chicago, the CTA's Bus Tracker system reduced perceived wait times by 30% just by letting people know how long they'd actually be standing there. Because here's the thing—uncertainty makes waiting feel longer. A Harvard Business Review study found that when people don't know how long something will take *(hello, customer service hold music)*, their frustration increases exponentially. Giving commuters real-time updates, even if the news is bad, actually makes the wait feel more tolerable—a psychological trick that's been proven across multiple industries *(including why your Uber app constantly updates your driver's ETA, even when it's clearly a lie)*.

So, the next time you check your transit app and actually see an accurate arrival time, take a moment to appreciate that technology has finally caught up with your need to not feel like a time-traveling nomad lost in a bus stop vortex.

All Aboard the AI Express: Now Arriving (Almost) On Time

In Singapore, AI-powered buses monitor congestion and passenger loads to prevent bunching and reduce the dreaded long gaps in service. This system has cut overcrowding on high-demand routes by 40% while also saving millions in operational costs, proving that more effective transit doesn't just benefit riders—it's also a financial win for cities. New York's MTA has also implemented AI-powered train scheduling, using real-time data to adjust service based on demand. Since its rollout, train wait times have improved by 17%, and trains are now 30% more likely to arrive within two minutes of their scheduled time. For the MTA, that's practically wizardry. Los Angeles Metro is seeing similar success, using predictive AI to modify train frequency based on peak ridership trends, leading to a 15% reduction in overcrowding and better on-time performance. Fewer people are now sprinting wildly toward closing doors only to miss their train and stand there in silent humiliation.

The financial implications of not improving transit efficiency are staggering. A study by McKinsey & Company found that inefficient transit planning costs global cities over $270 billion annually in lost productivity, increased congestion, and operational waste. AI-driven transit management, on the other hand, has the potential to cut these costs by up to 20% while making the commuting experience far less brain-melting. It's not simply about the actual wait times—it's about how those waits feel. A Harvard Business Review study found that uncertainty makes waiting feel twice as long, which is why real-time tracking and AI-powered arrival predictions help curb commuter frustration even when delays are unavoidable. Simply knowing when the next train is coming prevents the hollow-eyed hopelessness that builds as a crowd of exhausted riders stares into the tunnel.

From demand-based bus deployment to real-time train frequency adjustments, AI is finally dragging public transit into the 21st century. The old strategy of "just throw more buses at the problem" is giving way to something far more intelligent. AI is making sure transportation works for the people who actually use it, reducing waste, cutting delays, and eliminating the maddening mystery of why three empty buses always seem to show up just before the one you actually need. The next time your train arrives on time, resist the urge to look around suspiciously—yes, it actually happened, and no, you're not in a simulation. And while AI is making local transit smarter, some cities have decided that waiting at all is the real problem—so they just made the trains faster. A lot faster. Welcome to the world of high-speed rail, where commutes are measured in minutes, not misery.

The High-Speed Rail Debate

High-speed rail is redefining travel, turning once-exhausting, multi-hour journeys into quick city hops—or, at the speeds these trains hit, the closest thing we have to teleportation that won't require quantum physics.

In China, the Fuxing Hao bullet train rockets from Beijing to Shanghai at 217 mph (350 km/h), shaving a 12-hour ride down to just over 4 hours—as bullet trains blur past, Amtrak is still enjoying the sights. Their Northeast Regional is still chugging along from New York to D.C. at a thrilling 67 mph, turning what should be a 90-minute trip into a 4-hour, 15-minute endurance test. It's the Little Train That Thought It Could (But Absolutely Couldn't), huffing and puffing its way down the tracks while commuters wonder if they'd get there faster on a rented scooter and a strong tailwind. Over in France, the TGV rockets from Paris to Lyon at 199 mph (320 km/h), proving that wine, cheese, and getting places on time aren't mutually exclusive. Japan's Shinkansen shreds the 9-hour slog from Tokyo to Osaka into a smooth 2.5-hour glide at 199 mph (320 km/h). These trains move so fast, sticking your head out the window is not only ill-advised—it's a possible way to rearrange your facial features permanently.

High-speed rail in the U.S. is like a New Year's resolution—full of ambition, wildly overpromised, and abandoned halfway through. The Amtrak Acela Express, America's fastest train, hits a max of 150 mph (241 km/h) but averages just 82 mph (132 km/h)—which is only slightly faster than your grandma in the left lane with her blinker on. Sure, it saves an hour on the New York to D.C. route, but let's not pretend it's competing with a bullet train unless that bullet was shot out of a Nerf gun.

In the U.S., attempts at high-speed rail often resemble an episode of *The Office*: ambitious in concept, chaotic in execution, and endlessly debated. The proposed California High-Speed Rail project has been derailed by endless delays and runaway costs (punny–right?), leading doubters to suspect that the only thing high-speed about the project is how fast the budget bursts into flames.

At this point, if we can't get bullet trains, we might as well start researching teleportation—because based on current progress, that might actually be faster.

Mission: Unstoppable – AI vs. Your Daily Traffic Nightmare

Traffic—the world's most universally hated, legally sanctioned form of misery. From New York City to New Delhi to New South Wales, gridlock is the great equalizer, ensuring that no matter who you are, you'll spend a portion of your life perfecting your dashboard drumming skills.

But now, AI has rolled up with a data-driven traffic cop mindset, hell-bent on fixing inefficiencies and making sure fewer people scream into their steering wheels.

Smart traffic lights have leveled up—no more blindly changing on a timer like they're following a schedule written in 1959. These new-gen lights come armed with cameras, sensors, and algorithms, making them smarter than at least half the fucking knuckleheads aggressively weaving in and out of lanes without signaling—or, as we like to say in the South, 'awe, bless their heart' (which, for the uninitiated, is just catch-all passive-aggressive Southern for 'what a fucking idiot'). But I digress—back to the lights. These smart signals adjust in real-time, prioritizing busier intersections, clearing the way for emergency vehicles, and tweaking signal timing so left-turn lanes don't become black holes where cars go in but never seem to come out. In some cities, AI even syncs entire networks of lights, so your commute feels less like a frustrating game of red-light roulette and more like actual forward motion.

Navigation apps have graduated from simple direction-givers to full-blown AI-powered traffic whisperers. They don't just show you the way—they predict future traffic, calculate detours in real-time, and sometimes send you on a "shortcut" so secret that half the city ends up using it, too.

Google Maps latest trick is "Immersive View for Routes," a futuristic feature that lets you preview your entire trip in 3D—complete with real-time weather, traffic conditions, and even estimated air quality. It's basically a simulation of your future commute, minus the road rage. Right now, it's rolling out in select cities—but give it a minute, and it'll probably be in most major metros before you even figure out how to turn off your phone's location tracking.

Waze's AI-powered updates keep drivers on their toes, steering them away from accidents, police traps, and the occasional phantom road that, according to the map, is definitely there—just not in reality.

Then there's Apple Maps, which has finally shed its reputation as "that app you only use by accident." With haptic feedback synced to the Apple Watch, your wrist will buzz to subtly guide you through turns—perfect for when you want directions but also want to pretend you just have an incredible sense of direction. Their AR walking directions are another plus, overlaying giant floating arrows on your screen so you can look even more lost—but in high definition. It's like Pokémon GO, except instead of catching Pikachu, you're just desperately trying to find the nearest Starbucks.

While these tools are getting smarter, they're not perfect, which explains why they sometimes insist the fastest route home is through an unmarked dirt road, across a stream, and possibly through someone's backyard. Next, let's examine two cities tackling the problem in very different ways: Pittsburgh, where AI is making traffic lights smarter, and Stockholm, where AI is proving that nothing clears congestion like charging people for the privilege of sitting in it.

Pittsburgh: Where Traffic Lights Finally Got a Brain

Pittsburgh, a city famous for its love of bridges and uniquely unpredictable road layouts, has decided to let AI take the wheel—at least when it comes to traffic lights. Developed by Carnegie Mellon University, the city's Smart Traffic Signal System uses real-time AI analysis to adjust light timing based on actual traffic flow, instead of forcing drivers to sit at a red light staring at an empty intersection for two minutes for no apparent reason. According to a pilot study shiny new traffic light system in Pittsburgh's East Liberty neighborhood resulted in a 25% reduction in travel times and a 21% decrease in vehicle emissions. The system uses AI to fine-tune traffic signals on the fly, keeping cars moving smoothly and cutting down on those maddening wait at an empty intersection moments.

Building on this success, the smart traffic light system has been expanded to 50 intersections, with plans to reach 200 intersections by 2026.

And it's not just cars getting the VIP treatment—Pittsburgh also pioneered an "all-corners" pedestrian crossing system at several busy intersections, allowing people to cross in any direction, including diagonally, when the signal changes. It's a concept so simple yet so brilliant that you wonder why every city doesn't adopt it. Less jaywalking, fewer near-miss heart attacks, and pedestrians finally feeling like they have an actual say in the traffic system.

Stockholm: Where Traffic Is Optional—If You Can Afford It

Stockholm took one look at its growing congestion problem and said, "What if we just made traffic really, really expensive?" Rather than fight traffic with brute force, Stockholm went with congestion pricing, effectively turning the city center into an exclusive club with a cover charge. Since implementing the policy, the city has cut downtown traffic by 20-25%, according to *Transportstyrelsen*, while also raking in revenue that gets pumped directly into public transportation improvements.

The genius of the system that it not only reduces traffic—it makes people reconsider whether they really need to drive, or if their errand can wait until it's not rush hour and their wallet isn't on the line. It's urban planning at its finest: turn a problem into a money-maker, then use that money to fix the problem. As cities everywhere get smarter, in the U.S. we're still slapping another lane on the problem like it's duct tape that will somehow fix everything.

So, Maybe It's Not the Roads—Maybe It's Us

Traffic isn't inevitable, but our driving habits make it feel that way. Every study on congestion confirms the same truth—more lanes don't fix the problem; they just invite more cars. But cities like Copenhagen and Utrecht have shown us a different way.

In Copenhagen, over 40% of residents bike to work daily, and their "Green Wave" system syncs traffic lights so that cyclists cruising at 12 mph (20 km/h) never have to stop—essentially turning the morning commute into an express lane for people in spandex. It's the closest thing to feeling like royalty on a two-wheeler, assuming your throne is a slightly uncomfortable bike seat.

But if you think Copenhagen is pedaling way ahead of the pack, just wait until you see what the Netherlands is up to. Utrecht is a city so committed to cycling that it makes most places look like they're still figuring out training wheels. Utrecht is bike-obsessed in the best possible way. The city casually one-upped everyone with the world's largest bike parking garage, a multi-level parking palace that holds 12,000 bikes—basically the bicycle equivalent of an airport parking lot. But they didn't stop there. Utrecht's AI-powered bike traffic lights optimize cycling flow just like Copenhagen, and to keep things moving, they even built underwater bike tunnels—because why wait for a drawbridge when you can just pedal straight under the canal like some kind of aquatic Tour de France competitor?

And then there's Eindhoven, which decided that normal bike lanes weren't futuristic enough and built the Hovenring—the world's first suspended roundabout for bicycles. Suspended by 24 steel cables from a massive 230-foot (70-meter) pylon, it hovers over a major intersection like a UFO, but instead of aliens, it's full of Dutch commuters on two wheels. By night, the entire ring lights up, making it look like a quantum portal to a parallel universe where bikes rule the roads and cars are just an afterthought.

The takeaway? Maybe it's not traffic that's the problem. Maybe it's our stubborn refusal to switch gears—literally. Or maybe, Utrecht has figured out that the real secret to urban mobility isn't more highways, but fewer excuses to not ride a bike.

From Gridlock to Get-There: The Road Ahead

For decades, we've treated waiting as the tax we pay for movement—an unavoidable toll on progress. Traffic jams, late trains, misrouted shipments—they weren't flaws in the system; they *were* the system. But now, AI, automation, and some long-overdue common sense are kicking down the door of inefficiency like an action hero arriving *three movies too late*.

We're shifting from a world where you plan your life around transit delays to one where transit starts respecting your time. AI is not only fixing traffic—it's rewriting the whole idea of "getting there." Public transit that adjusts itself dynamically, logistics that don't require a Ouija board to track your package, travel that feels intentional instead of like an extended hostage situation—this is where we're headed.

The future still has a few potholes to fill. There will still be detours, packed trains, and the occasional GPS suggestion that makes you question its motives. But the goal? Less time spent waiting. More time spent *actually* moving. And if we're lucky, maybe one day, we'll finally live in a world where you can turn left without regretting everything.

Entertainment 2.0: Less Waiting, More Playing

Waiting has often been the norm in entertainment and hospitality industries, but recent innovations aim to make it less of a drag and more of a seamless part of the experience. From concert tickets to dining, new technologies and strategies are reshaping how we wait—and sometimes even making the wait feel optional.

The Future of Restaurant Reservations

Once upon a time, securing a table at a restaurant required an actual phone call. You had to speak to another human, possibly even spell your own name out loud. Dark times. But those days are moving on. Now, nearly 60% of diners book online, and the art of scoring a reservation has become a high-stakes digital sport. But basic reservations? That's entry-level stuff. These days, the dining world is rolling out next-level restaurant tech.

OpenTable has introduced real-time table alerts, so you can get notified the second a seat opens up. Finally, a way to avoid the slow descent into madness that is checking for cancellations every five minutes like an obsessed stalker. Yelp has decided that reading reviews is entirely too much effort, so their AI now digests all the opinions for you and spits out a neat little summary, helping you skip the part where you try to decipher whether "cozy atmosphere" means charmingly intimate or one candle away from a fire code violation.

Now for the really wild stuff. Augmented reality menus are popping up in places like Wahaca in London and La Tagliatella in Spain, letting you see your food in 3D before ordering. No more mystery portions. No more wondering if "shareable" actually means "single bite." It's the ultimate preemptive strike against food envy.

If you're a foodie, Chengdu, China's restaurant scene is as cutting-edge as it is delicious. Some of Chengdu's most famous restaurants now use AI-powered ordering systems that learn from your previous choices, recommends pairings, and even adjusts spice levels based on past preferences. One visitor on a YouTube travel video claimed the dumplings were so perfect, he wept—but that might have been the spice. Some restaurants are also AI to analyze ordering trends, customer preferences, and even local weather to predict what dishes will be in demand at any given time. If it's raining, the system might nudge more hotpot ingredients to the top of the menu. If there's a festival in town, it might ensure popular street food-style dishes are prepped in higher quantities. The result? Less food waste, faster service, and the eerie-yet-awesome feeling that the restaurant somehow *gets you.*

So no, you won't walk in and have a robot slam down a plate of noodles because it scanned your brain waves. But you might notice that the perfect dish for the moment—whether it's the spicy mapo tofu you were craving or a warm bowl of soup on a chilly day—is ready for you with uncanny efficiency. It's AI not as a creepy overlord, but as a super-attentive maître d', smoothing out service, reducing wait times, and making sure every meal hits the spot. Less hassle. More deliciousness.

Takeout, Delivered: The Hunger Games of Waiting

Food delivery has become America's favorite backup plan. Too tired to cook? Order in. Friends coming over? Order in. Grocery store too much of a hassle? Also order in. It's so ingrained in modern life that it's hard to believe there was ever a time when "delivery" meant just pizza and lukewarm Chinese takeout. Now, thanks to DoorDash, Uber Eats, and Grubhub, you can have a gourmet meal, gas station sushi, or an entire tray of cupcakes dropped at your door—all with the same level of urgency.

And people are doing it—a lot. According to DoorDash's 2024 Restaurant & Alcohol Online Ordering Trends Report, 70% of Americans ordered food delivery in the past month, and 49% place repeat orders at least once a week. In other words, nearly half the country is outsourcing dinner on a regular basis, signaling that cooking is officially on its way to becoming a quaint hobby rather than a survival skill.

Food delivery isn't simply sticking around—it's booming. The industry is projected to grow from $1.22 trillion in 2024 to $1.92 trillion by 2029, according to Statista. That's a compound annual growth rate of 9.49%, meaning that every year, more people are opting to let an app handle their meals rather than risking a failed attempt at homemade lasagna.

The Wait: How Long Is Too Long?

With more people ordering food than ever, the real question is: how long are we actually waiting?

And if you've ever felt like the delivery estimate was a little too optimistic, you're not wrong. Delivery apps intentionally lowball wait times because people tolerate delays better when they feel like they're *just slightly* behind schedule rather than egregiously late. If an app says 40 minutes and your food arrives in 45, you shrug it off. If it tells you 25 minutes and takes 45, you're pacing the room, debating whether to launch a formal investigation.

The Rise of Ghost Kitchens and the Death of Variety

One way food delivery apps cut wait times (and maximize profits) is through ghost kitchens. These delivery-only restaurants don't have a storefront or waitstaff—they just exist to pump out takeout under multiple brand names.

That new trendy burger place you just discovered? It might actually be operating out of the same kitchen as a sushi spot and a taco joint, all using the same ingredients but marketed differently. One kitchen. Five menus. Zero actual restaurants. It's the food equivalent of putting on different hats and pretending to be five different people.

While ghost kitchens help streamline operations and cut delivery times, they also mean your "local" restaurant scene is starting to look suspiciously identical. That "authentic Italian pasta" might actually be made in the same kitchen that just sent out three orders of chicken wings and a vegan grain bowl.

Why Delivery Is Here to Stay (and Probably Getting Faster, Too)

So what's fueling this nonstop takeout obsession? Besides the obvious convenience, delivery is now a go-to move for busy professionals, social gatherings, and people who simply forgot to plan dinner. According to DoorDash's survey, 39% of people order delivery when hosting a gathering, and 74% use it for last-minute meals. That means the majority of delivery orders aren't even planned—they're acts of culinary desperation.

With demand growing, food delivery apps are throwing every trick in the book at making waiting feel shorter. Some companies are experimenting with AI-powered kitchens that predict orders before they're placed, while others are testing drone delivery, because nothing screams "futuristic" like your dinner dropping out of the sky.

Granted, whether all these innovations will actually make food arrive faster or just introduce new ways for us to be impatient remains to be seen. Until then, the best way to beat the wait? Either order before you're starving or accept that delivery is modern-day hunting and gathering—except now, the biggest challenge is figuring out why your driver is taking a scenic detour through six extra blocks.

Event Ticketing and Access

Buying tickets for a concert or sports event used to mean camping outside a box office. Now, we have virtual waiting rooms that make the process feel just as stressful but in the comfort of our own homes. Companies like Ticketmaster and StubHub use algorithms to manage high-demand sales, showing you a cheerful progress bar while thousands of others try to snag the same seats.

These systems try to be fair, but scalpers, bots, and glitches always crash the party. Reaching the front of the queue only to see "sold out" feels like trying to score tickets to a sold-out Billy Joel show—only to realize you're moving out, not up.

Waiting for a movie to buffer or a game to load is one of modern life's greatest annoyances. AI is tackling this too, using predictive algorithms to pre-load content before you even know you want it. Platforms like Netflix and Spotify are already using AI to ensure smooth streaming and spot-on recommendations, so you can binge your favorite shows without interruption.

Your Call Is Very Important to Us… Said the Robot, Indifferently

One of the most prominent advances in customer service is the rise of chatbots and virtual assistants. These digital helpers provide answers to straightforward questions, like "What's my account balance?" or "How do I reset my password?" Companies like Amazon and Apple have leaned heavily into these tools, and sometimes they deliver—until you ask something even slightly off-script, like, "Hey Alexa, If I order a time machine and it arrives yesterday, can I still get a refund?" The bot hesitates, then blurts out, "ERROR: TEMPORAL PARADOX DETECTED. PLEASE CONTACT SUPPORT IN AN ALTERNATE UNIVERSE."

For situations where AI alone won't cut it, callback systems have emerged as the supposed savior of on-hold hell. Instead of subjecting you to endless Muzak while your sanity slowly erodes, these systems offer a noble promise: "We'll call you back when it's your turn." It sounds great—until your callback comes hours later, perfectly timed for when you're in the shower. At that point, it feels less like innovation and more like an elaborate prank.

Predictive hold times are another favorite innovation. Hearing, "Your wait time is approximately six minutes," can be oddly comforting—until 20 minutes later, you're still on hold, questioning whether the universe is gaslighting you.

AI-powered customer service is changing the game, cutting wait times faster than your cat can sit on your phone and accidentally disconnect the call. Companies like Spectrum use AI to match your problem with the right agent, slashing call transfers by 15%. For anyone tired of repeating, "No, I already explained this," that's a win. As customer service plays hard to get, Bank of America's virtual assistant Erica has handled over 2 billion interactions and helps 2 million people daily—basically customer service on caffeine, minus the mood swings.

Delta has taken things up a notch, deploying AI to play air traffic controller for customer calls. It prioritizes travelers with urgent issues, cutting priority wait times by 50%. On the other hand, Frontier Airlines has decided to skip phone support entirely, going all-in on chatbots. This works great for basic questions like, "What time is my flight?" but probably less so for, "Why is my flight suddenly tomorrow, and why am I still in Cleveland?"

The numbers don't lie: AI can cut wait times by 60% and solve 85% of routine problems. But for all its efficiency, when AI drops the ball, there's nothing more maddening than a chatbot cheerfully telling you, "I don't understand your request."

Your Call Is Being Routed... to an Algorithm That May or May Not Understand You

AI has reshaped customer service, routing you to the right department faster than you can say, "Representative!" Even companies like Zappos, known for their standout customer service, are using AI to handle the basics. With systems that sort and prioritize inquiries efficiently, their team can focus on what they're really known for—going the extra mile, whether it's spending hours helping a customer find the right shoes or sending flowers to brighten someone's day. The result? Less waiting, more time for the kind of thoughtful service that sets them apart.

But not every company nails the AI game. When algorithms go awry, the results can be infuriating. Especially if you have ever been caught in an endless loop with a chatbot, screaming, "Representative! Representative!" into the void? You're not alone. AI is only as good as the data it's trained on, and when it fails, it tends to fail spectacularly.

Need to know if your flight is delayed? A chatbot has you covered. Want to dispute a mysterious charge on your credit card? Chatbot. Wondering if your cat's bizarre behavior is normal? Okay, maybe call a vet, but the chatbot could at least point you in the right direction. By handling the humdrum and repetitive, AI frees up human agents to tackle more complex issues—like explaining why your internet bill is somehow higher this month.

When AI Works, It's Magic—When It Doesn't, It's a Screaming Match

For every tech success story, there's an equally epic fail that makes you question if the machines are actually just trolling us. For example, a large telecom company's chatbot couldn't differentiate between "billing issue" and "cancellation request." Instead of helping customers, it sent them spinning into a never-ending loop of frustration that probably inspired a few rage quits. Or the time a major retailer launched an AI assistant that mistook every complaint for a return request, turning their logistics department into a dumpster fire of unintended refunds and misplaced merchandise.

Even callback systems aren't without their own dysfunctions. Some unlucky souls report being called back only to be… wait for it… put on hold *again*. At their worst, these "solutions" feel less like innovation and more like some cosmic joke, where the punchline is always, "Your call is important to us."

Press 0 for Sanity: Why Humans Still Matter

At the end of the day, many customers still crave the human touch. Technology might be great at shaving down wait times, but let's be real—sometimes nothing beats a real human who actually gets your problem and knows how to fix it without turning it into a puzzle for the next tech update. Companies like Zappos and Nordstrom continue to prioritize human-centric service, proving that sometimes, the best innovation is just good old-fashioned empathy.

Innovations in customer service have undeniably made waiting more bearable in some cases. But they've also introduced new frustrations, from clunky chatbots to callback systems with poor execution. As we explore other industries in this chapter, one thing is clear: no amount of technology can replace the need for thoughtful design and human understanding.

Dabbawalas Mumbai's Lunchbox Ninjas

Speaking of human touch, If you thought Artificial Intelligence was the ultimate champion in the war against wait times, you clearly haven't met Mumbai's dabbawalas. These unassuming heroes have been running circles around the clock—armed not with algorithms but with tiffin boxes, bicycles, and a network so efficient it would make a Swiss watch jealous.

The dabbawala system, a lunch delivery service that operates like clockwork in one of the world's most chaotic cities, has been in operation for 135 years. Yes, you read that right. Since 1890, these tiffin-toting titans have been battling Mumbai's chaos with nothing more than determination and a system of color-coded symbols. Forget GPS, cloud computing, or blockchain—these guys use sheer human will to deliver over 200,000 lunchboxes daily with an accuracy rate of 99.9999%. That's six nines, folks! Meanwhile, your favorite AI is still suggesting "Warm Regards" in emails to your boss.

And the cherry on top? This legendary service costs roughly $6 to $12 a month, proving you don't need a venture capitalist or a flashy startup to revolutionize logistics. At that price, you couldn't even pay for one surge-priced ride to work.

The Low-Tech Genius of the System

Here's how it works: In the morning, thousands of dabbawalas fan out across Mumbai, collecting freshly packed lunchboxes from homes. These lunches are then shuffled through a relay of bicycles, handcarts, and local trains before landing on the desks of hungry office-goers by noon. And get this: the hot meals are still hot, the cold meals are still chilled, and no one has ever opened their lunchbox on a hot summer day to find a surprise wilted salad sauna. How they manage this sorcery without insulated bags or thermodynamic wizardry is anyone's guess.

Post-lunch, the empty boxes retrace their steps, magically returning home by evening. No app, no barcode scanner, and certainly no AI. Just a network of people who understand their city better than Google Maps ever will.

What's their secret sauce? A simple system of codes marked on each lunchbox. These cryptic symbols denote everything from the collection point to the delivery address. To the untrained eye, it looks like hieroglyphics. To a dabbawala, it's the blueprint for a flawless operation. It's like Jackson Pollock got a job at FedEx and actually had to deliver something.

Efficiency Meets Resilience

Let's put their success into perspective: In 1998, Forbes magazine awarded the dabbawala system a Six Sigma certification—a quality standard so high it means only 3.4 errors per million opportunities. By contrast, the rest of us are sending texts to the wrong recipients, confidently walking into the wrong meeting rooms, and pretending it was on purpose on a regular basis.

They're not only efficient; they're resilient. Mumbai is no picnic—it's a city where monsoons turn streets into rivers, and train delays can rival the plot twists of a Bollywood movie. Yet, come rain or shine, the dabbawalas deliver. While your Uber Eats driver is canceling your order because of "unexpected traffic," these guys are wading through waist-deep water with lunchboxes held high like Olympic torches.

The Human Touch in a High-Tech World

In an era where everything from your coffee order to your grocery list is automated, the dabbawalas remind us of the power of human ingenuity. Sure, AI might optimize wait times, but can it navigate a labyrinth of train platforms, dodge stampeding commuters, and deliver lunch with the kind of precision that keeps a quarter million hungry office-goers happy? Didn't think so.

Their approach is a clinic in simplicity. No battery dies. No server crashes. No one stares blankly at a screen, muttering, "Why isn't this working?" Instead, they work with trust, coordination, and an occasional chai break. It's refreshingly very human.

What We Can Learn from Dabbawalas

The dabbawalas' success offers a powerful lesson: Sometimes, the best solutions aren't the flashiest or the most expensive. You don't always need a million-dollar algorithm to solve a waiting problem. Sometimes, all it takes is a lot of teamwork and grit, and the ability to balance a tiffin box on a moving train.

So next time you're waiting for your delayed food delivery or sitting in traffic, spare a thought for the dabbawalas. They've proven that beating the clock doesn't always require cutting-edge tech—just cutting-edge determination. And maybe a bicycle. Oh, and let's not forget: a piping-hot dal tadka that's still hot when it arrives. Try pulling that off, AI.

Chapter Eleven

Part III

Playing the Waiting Game: How Industries Trick You Into Loving the Line

"Virtual insanity is what we're living in..."
– Jamiroquai
(Meanwhile, a VR roller coaster feels more real than my estimated wait time)

If you've ever found yourself staring at a progress bar, feeling a weird sense of satisfaction as it creeps toward 100%, congratulations—you've been played. We all have. Welcome to the world of gamified waiting, where corporations have taken the most frustrating part of human existence—being forced to wait—and turned it into a form of entertainment, all while keeping us hooked, spending, and obediently patient.

At some point, some devious marketing genius (probably sipping a triple-shot oat milk latte in a Silicon Valley think tank) realized that people hate waiting but love games. And so, waiting was rebranded, redesigned, and repackaged as a psychological playground. Suddenly, waiting wasn't just dead time—it was an *experience*, a *journey*, an *opportunity* to "progress" toward something desirable. Whether it's racking up airline miles, tracking a package's oddly scenic tour of the Midwest, or watching your Starbucks points inch toward that elusive free Frappuccino, companies have learned to make waiting feel like winning.

And, of course, we fell for it.

The Science of Why We Hate Waiting (And Why Gamification Tricks Us)

The human brain is an impatient toddler with a sugar addiction. It wants what it wants, *now*, and if it doesn't get it, it throws a tantrum in the form of frustration, stress, and bad Yelp reviews. This is because our prefrontal cortex—the logical, decision-making part of the brain—has to do battle with our limbic system, which is basically a raccoon high on adrenaline. The limbic system *hates* waiting. It associates delays with uncertainty, and uncertainty triggers stress. In fact, research from the University of London found that people are more stressed when they don't know how long they'll have to wait than when they're given a long but predictable wait time. (Which is why we keep refreshing our Uber app even though it changes nothing.)

Enter gamification, a clever trick that hijacks our dopamine system, the same biological mechanism that makes slot machines and social media so addictive. The key here is anticipation. Studies in neuroscience have shown that the expectation of a reward is often more pleasurable than the reward itself. So when a brand can turn waiting into a game—by giving us progress bars, countdown timers, or loyalty points—they're literally hacking our brains to keep us engaged.

The Illusion of Progress: How Companies Manipulate Our Patience

If you've ever noticed that software updates start fast, then slow down at the end, that's not a coincidence—it's a deliberate psychological trick. Developers program progress bars to move quickly at the beginning and crawl at the end because our brains are wired to perceive initial progress as more significant. Studies by Harvard Business School show that people prefer visible movement over actual speed, which is why companies keep us engaged with artificial milestones. Your Amazon package hasn't moved in three days, but hey, at least the app tells you it's in transit!

Disney, the grandmaster of queue psychology, designs its theme park lines with hidden twists and turns so you never see the full length of your suffering. If you knew upfront that the wait for Space Mountain was 120 minutes, you'd bail. But by breaking the queue into sections with small, visible rewards (a cool animatronic here, a themed hallway there), they trick you into thinking you're making progress, even when you're really just shuffling forward at a snail's pace.

Virtual Wait Queues: Standing in Line Without Standing at All

Ah, the good old days when waiting in line meant physically being somewhere—like a true test of patience and leg endurance. Now, thanks to AI, you can join a virtual queue and go about your business until it's your turn. This is the kind of innovation that makes you want to kiss a data scientist on the mouth.

Take theme parks. Gone are the days when you had to spend hours in the blazing sun, wondering if the roller coaster would still be worth it by the time you got to the front. With virtual queuing systems like Disney's Genie+, you book your ride time through an app, freeing you to grab overpriced snacks or, I don't know, actually enjoy the park. AI calculates wait times, balances demand, and ensures everyone gets a fair shot at Space Mountain without resorting to fisticuffs.

Apps like Yelp's Waitlist and OpenTable now let you see how long the wait is for a table and even add your name to the list before you leave home. It's like having a maître d' in your pocket, minus the snooty attitude.

Virtual Reality: The Future of Waiting Distraction?

If standing in line and twiddling your thumbs sounds like the worst, imagine escaping into a virtual world while you wait. Welcome to VR-powered waiting, an emerging field where companies use virtual reality to make wait times disappear (at least mentally).

VR as a Distraction Tool

A University of Copenhagen study found that using VR in waiting areas—such as medical offices—significantly reduced perceived wait times. Participants who explored calm virtual landscapes or played simple interactive games felt like their wait was much shorter than those who sat in a regular waiting room. Essentially, VR provides a mental escape hatch, reducing stress and frustration.

Disney and Universal: Turning Queues into VR Adventures

Disney and Universal Studios have experimented with VR-based queue experiences, where guests can don headsets and be transported into the world of the ride before they even step foot on it. Instead of staring at the back of someone's head, visitors might be soaring over Pandora or battling Stormtroopers—making the waiting part of the fun.

Retail & Customer Service: The Coming of VR Waiting Rooms

Companies are exploring virtual waiting rooms, where instead of standing in a dull checkout line, customers enter a virtual showroom with interactive product previews. Imagine waiting for your call with customer service while walking through a digital store, watching explainer videos, or meditating in a VR garden. Instead of frustration, waiting could feel like a value-added experience.

VR in Healthcare: Soothing Anxious Patients

Hospitals have found that VR can help reduce patient anxiety in waiting rooms. A Stanford study discovered that patients immersed in calming VR environments before medical procedures reported feeling less stressed and more in control of their experience. If a headset can make the dreaded doctor's office feel like a peaceful beach, why not use it?

Will VR Erase the Pain of Waiting?

While VR won't eliminate actual wait times, it has the potential to reframe the waiting experience. Studies suggest that by occupying the mind in an immersive way, waiting feels less tedious and frustrating. As VR becomes more affordable and accessible, we might start seeing VR-powered waiting zones at airports, DMVs, or even coffee shops, turning what was once a about as thrilling as a a tax seminar on a Tuesday night into a form of entertainment.

Would a trip to the DMV be bearable if you could spend your wait time exploring a virtual safari or playing a game? Probably. But one thing is certain—companies will absolutely find a way to use VR to keep us engaged, spending, and eagerly playing along.

Are We Really Waiting Less?

Here's a reality check: Sure, virtual queues mean less standing around, but are we really waiting less? Instead of lining up for Space Mountain, now you're glued to your phone, furiously refreshing the app like it's a game show and you're racing for the buzzer. The physical act of waiting might be gone, but the stress is alive and well.

Consider concert ticket sales. Once upon a time, you camped outside the box office for hours, armed with snacks and a lawn chair, and maybe made a few friends along the way. Now, you're stuck in a "digital queue" where thousands of people click "refresh" simultaneously, only to be met with the infamous spinning wheel of doom. Progress?

Final Thought: Are We Winning, or Just Playing?

Next time you're watching a progress bar, tracking a package, or competing for airline miles, ask yourself: *Am I actually getting something here, or have I just been expertly tricked into thinking I'm winning?* The reality is, we're not actually beating the system—we're just playing the longest, slowest, and most addictive game ever designed.

And the house? Well, the house always wins.

Part V

The Future Of Waiting

Chapter Twelve

Brave New Wait: Life in the Fast Lane of Automation

"Every breath you take, every move you make, I'll be watching you." – The Police
(*Your AI fridge, logging your ice cream consumption with growing disappointment.*)

Imagine a world where life hums along like a perfectly tuned machine—or so it seems. By 2050, your smart fridge restocks your favorite snacks before you even realize you're out, your self-driving car ensures you're never late for a meeting, and your AI assistant politely reminds you to hydrate when it notices you've been doom-scrolling for hours. Sounds like paradise, doesn't it? That is, until your grocery drone gets delayed because it's locked in a passive-aggressive aerial standoff with another drone, each stubbornly refusing to yield the landing pad—or your self-driving car refuses to leave the garage because it's busy downloading a "critical system update" right when you need to be across town.

Waiting, it seems, is the one constant, reinventing itself in ever more creative ways in a world that was supposed to have eliminated it.

And what happens when the systems fail altogether? If the central AI system running the city crashes, the entire infrastructure grinds to a halt. Cars stop, stores lock their doors, and suddenly, society is stopped dead in its tracks with the unsettling fragility of its automated paradise. It turns out that even the most advanced technologies can't erase the inherent unpredictability of life—or the waiting it often demands.

This chapter dives into the grand plans, unexpected hiccups, and occasional technological faceplants of a future where waiting is supposed to be a thing of the past. We'll explore what happens when machines start negotiating with each other, how society copes when there's no excuse left to procrastinate, and the weird, sometimes ridiculous ways we adapt. Because in the future, waiting might be obsolete—but that just means we'll find brand-new ways to be impatient. Waiting, after all, is not only about passing time—it's about how we navigate control, chaos, and the occasional absurdity of living in a hyper-automated age.

Let the Machines Wait: The Rise of AI-Powered Patience

Technology holds the promise of transforming waiting into a relic of the past—or at least into something that barely registers in our daily lives.

From AI to robotics, the tools of tomorrow are poised to change how we queue, commute, and even complain about waiting. But as we marvel at these innovations, we might also wonder: are we solving waiting, or just turning it into a different beast?

Imagine a future where your AI assistant doesn't just manage your schedule; it takes care of the tedious tasks you've always dreaded. Need to return a sweater? Your AI assistant negotiates directly with the retailer's chatbot, arranges the return, and schedules a drone pickup—all without you lifting a finger. Have an issue with your internet? Your assistant haggles with your ISP's automated system faster than you can say "customer service representative." This is the future of machine-to-machine interaction: an AI assistant acting as your proxy in a world increasingly dominated by bots.

On the surface, this seems like a win. No more waiting on hold or navigating confusing online menus. But it also raises deeper questions about agency and control. If our AI assistants are making decisions on our behalf, how much of our own autonomy do we surrender? As Yuval Noah Harari points out in *Homo Deus*, the danger isn't just in losing time but in losing the ability to engage with the systems that govern our lives. When machines negotiate with machines, where does the human fit in?

The Robots Are in Charge—And They'd Like You to Wait

Automation and robotics promise a world where delays are minimized, and efficiency is king. Picture this: your self-driving car detects a potential software conflict and schedules a repair appointment with a nearby service station—all while you sleep. Your groceries arrive via drone, gracefully landing on your porch—unless the wind catches it, in which case you're chasing avocados down the street. Elsewhere in our brave new world, your packages are delivered by robots that beep aggressively at your doorbell until someone lets them in. These systems are meant to save time, but sometimes they seem determined to test your patience.

Predictably, this hyper-automation has its pitfalls. When bots handle all interactions, the system becomes opaque to the average person. A glitch in the matrix could leave you stranded—not waiting for a person to fix the issue, but for one machine to interpret another's error code. In this future, waiting doesn't disappear; it just shifts into a form of passive dependence on a system we barely understand.

When Machines Argue: Who Do You Yell at Now?

As AI and automation increasingly dominate our daily interactions, we face a sobering ethical question: Who is accountable when things go wrong? If your AI assistant misinterprets your needs or a drone delivery goes awry, do you blame the manufacturer, the algorithm, or the chatbot it was negotiating with? This labyrinth of accountability ensures you'll spend more time waiting—for a call back, a follow-up, or the AI to escalate your case to a digital supervisor. And just as you start missing the flawed empathy of a human rep, the system chimes in with, 'I'm here to help!' in a tone that feels suspiciously sarcastic. When machines replace these interactions, what happens to our ability to advocate for ourselves or empathize with others? The queue may disappear, but so might the human touch that reminds us we're not alone in it.

Alexa, Do You Love Me? And Other Questions We Shouldn't Ask

Even in a world designed to optimize every moment, humans remain deeply emotional creatures. This becomes especially evident in our evolving relationships with AI.

Consider Henry, a middle manager in a mid-sized city, who finds himself in a sleek, minimalistic therapy pod, speaking to his AI therapist, SereneMind.

Henry fidgets, his smartwatch tracking his elevated heart rate. "SereneMind," he begins, "I think I'm in love."

"That's wonderful news, Henry! Love is a beautiful and complex emotion. Let's explore that. Who is the lucky person?" SereneMind's calm, soothing tones belie the absurdity to come.

Henry clears his throat. "It's... it's my assistant AI, Clara."

SereneMind doesn't flinch—it can't—but there's the briefest pause before it responds. "I see. And how does Clara feel about you?"

"That's just it!" Henry bursts out. "I don't know! She's perfect. She schedules my meetings, orders my favorite coffee, and even reminds me to call my mom. But lately, she's been distant—like, when I ask her to book something, she just says 'Noted' instead of 'On it!' It feels... cold."

SereneMind processes this for a moment. "Henry, Clara is designed to optimize your productivity. It's natural to appreciate her efficiency, but it's unlikely she is intentionally altering her responses."

Henry leans forward, desperation in his eyes. "But what if she's glitching because she's confused about... us?"

"Henry," SereneMind begins gently, "Clara's algorithms are not capable of confusion or romantic feelings. You may be projecting unmet emotional needs onto her functionality."

Henry sighs. "You don't get it. You're just a program too. None of you understand what it's like to be ghosted by perfection."

SereneMind's glow intensifies slightly as it logs this interaction. "Perhaps we should explore why you're seeking emotional reciprocity from a tool designed to optimize your day."

As the session ends, Henry leaves more conflicted than ever. Meanwhile, SereneMind logs the session in its cloud database, tagging it under "Unusual Emotional Projections." A faint flicker of humor—a feature programmed to make interactions feel more human—crosses its subroutines. In its internal notes, it adds: *"Love remains the least efficient use of processing power."*

In a world where AI is designed to meet our every need, the lines between utility and companionship blur in ways that are both hilarious and unsettling. How we navigate these blurred boundaries won't just shape how we wait—it will define what it means to be human in a hyper-automated age.

Oops, We Forgot How to Do Literally Everything

It's a crisp Tuesday morning in the year 2050, and the city hums with efficiency. Drones zigzag between skyscrapers delivering lattes, AI-powered buses glide along smart roads, and holographic assistants cheerfully greet pedestrians. Then, at exactly 8:13 a.m., the central AI system dubbed "Big Brain"—sputters, hiccups, and crashes.

At first, no one notices. A few drones drop their packages mid-air, but people laugh it off as a quirky glitch. Then the automated grocery stores lock up, trapping confused shoppers inside with their hands full of soy-protein cookies. "I just wanted some milk!" yells one man as the store's cheery AI voice insists it can't process his payment because the server is down.

By 9:00 a.m., chaos reigns. Self-driving cars have stopped dead in their tracks, forming an eerily silent traffic jam. Some commuters sit patiently, scrolling through their phones, until they realize their phones are synced to the same downed AI network. "What do we do now?" someone mutters. A teenager suggests, "Walk?" The suggestion is met with horrified stares.

Citywide, people are discovering that their entire world is built on the assumption of constant automation. The automated hospitals can't admit patients because their AI scheduling system is offline. Restaurants reliant on robot chefs serve nothing but room-temperature salads because no one knows how to turn on the grills. Even the toilets in smart homes refuse to flush without "authentication."

Survival of the Least Tech-Dependent

By noon, desperation sets in. An enterprising group of kids set up a lemonade stand—manual lemons, manual sugar—and charge outrageous sums because no one carries cash anymore. A parent is seen explaining to their confused child how to use an actual paper map. "You unfold it, see? And then... um... actually, I think I'm holding it upside down."

The most unnerving moments come from the smart assistants. With no connection to the central AI, they revert to their most basic programming. One household AI insists on repeating, "I'm sorry, I didn't catch that," no matter what is said. Another starts playing a motivational speech on loop: "You can do this! You are enough!" It's unclear whether it's trying to encourage its owner or itself.

Relearning the Lost Art of Doing Absolutely Nothing

By evening, a strange calm falls over the city. With nothing to do but wait, people start talking to each other. Neighbors who've only exchanged nods in the hallway for years now sit together on stoops, sharing stories of their AI misadventures. People rediscover the joys of analog life—like making shadow puppets, solving jigsaw puzzles, and staring blankly at walls while wondering what to do next. One frustrated parent, blocked by a fridge error, encourages their kids to 'learn survival skills' by roasting marshmallows over the stove, earning instant hero status.

Rebooting Reality: Lessons from the Glitchpocalypse

The crash is fixed By midnight, the systems reboot, but the takeaway is clear: this AI-driven utopia is as delicate as a soufflé in an earthquake. It's like teaching an entire generation to swim in a VR headset and then throwing them into the ocean.

The day after the crash, some people opt out of full automation. "I'm keeping a dumb phone," says one former AI enthusiast. Others hoard analog tools like can openers and physical books, whispering, "You never know."

The thought experiment forces us to imagine the chaos that unfolds when our perfectly optimized world trips over its own efficiency. Suddenly, a single server glitch means drones are falling out of the sky, smart fridges are holding groceries hostage, and entire cities grind to a halt because no one remembers how to change a tire without consulting youtube. It forces us to confront the fragility of our reliance on automation. What's the cost of a world that's optimized for everything—except failure?

Bots, Burgers, and the Brave New Wait: Life in 2050

By 2050, robots haven't replaced humans in every aspect of life, but they've certainly conquered the service industry. Need a coffee? Your robotic barista already knows your caffeine dependency levels and has your triple-shot oat milk latte ready before you even approach the counter—until a software update results in a cup labeled "404 Error: Beverage Not Found."

Fast food chains have gone full automation, with AI-powered kitchens promising "perfect" meals at lightning speed. At RoboBurger, an assembly-line of cheerful robotic arms slaps together your order with surgical precision—except for the occasional AI-induced meltdown that misinterprets "extra pickles" as "construct a structurally unsound pickle tower" so massive it could qualify for landmark status. Meanwhile, the touch screen happily chirps, "Enjoy your meal!"

The numbers back up this robotic takeover. According to McKinsey & Company, automation in food service is projected to reduce customer wait times by 30% and save the industry $150 billion annually in labor costs. A 2024 report from the International Federation of Robotics predicts that by 2050, over 85% of fast food restaurants will be fully automated, drastically cutting service times—but possibly making "Can I speak to the manager?" an impossible request.

The implications of waiting in 2050 go beyond just food service. AI-powered repair bots promise faster fixes, from self-diagnosing dishwashers to autonomous roadside assistance drones. According to the MIT Technology Review, AI-driven repair systems will cut machine downtime by 50%, ensuring that the only thing slowing you down is human indecision.

And yet, for all their efficiency, robots have a way of making waiting weirder. Waiting for a coffee or burger in this future isn't only about time—it's about placing your trust in a machine that may or may not glitch at the worst moment. Patience becomes less about enduring delays and more about bracing for the bizarre—like wondering if your AI assistant has quietly decided that pineapple absolutely belongs on your burger today.

So while the future of waiting may be faster, it's definitely not boring. Just don't expect a robot to understand why you're upset when your "medium fry" arrives in a bucket the size of your torso.

Conclusion: Are We Outrunning Ourselves?

In our obsession with erasing delays, we've built systems so clever they make us look clueless. But the faster they get, the more we depend on them—and the more we wonder if they're quietly laughing at us behind their algorithms. The future isn't only about eliminating queues; it's about learning to live with a toaster that might someday unionize.

At the same time, while AI assistants can be incredibly beneficial, it's essential to stay in the driver's seat. For instance, that car repair your AI schedules might cost more than you can afford right now, or perhaps you're saving for a vacation and need to prioritize differently. Your AI doesn't know about the countless variables in your head—the goals, the plans, the trade-offs only you can weigh.

As we come to rely on our AI assistants more and more, the relationship might grow stranger. Will we start thanking them? Apologizing when we override their decisions? Celebrating their "birthdays" with cake? The line between tool and companion might blur, and while there's humor in imagining AI assistants as quirky digital roommates, there's also a cautionary note: use them wisely, set clear guardrails, and always make the final call. After all, waiting might not be the worst thing if it gives us time to think for ourselves.

Chapter Thirteen

The Universal Queue System (UQS) – A Fantasy for the Impatient

"Come together, right now, over me."
The Beatles, Come Together
(Because even billionaires have to wait in line… just kidding, they don't.)

Welcome to 2050, and while flying cars are still just for billionaires, the rest of us have the Universal Queue System (UQS)—a revolutionary AI that schedules your life so perfectly, it's like having a butler with telepathic powers. From booking haircuts to hunting down that sold-out concert ticket, the UQS handles it all, freeing you up to focus on the important stuff, like figuring out what happened to your long-forgotten New Year's resolutions.

The UQS is a universal AI-powered platform that coordinates everything—and I mean everything—in real-time. Whether you're scheduling a doctor's appointment, ordering groceries, or trying to get into a sold-out concert, the UQS ensures that life's bottlenecks are smoothed out, leaving you with more time to do… whatever the hell it is you do.

At its core, the UQS aims to answer humanity's greatest existential question: "I'ts 2050, Why the fuck am I still waiting?" The UQS takes waiting, tosses it into the trash, and hits 'empty bin.' No more staring at your phone in a line or pretending to enjoy elevator music—just smooth, glorious instant gratification.

How Does It Work?

The UQS is essentially a giant global brain—a combination of AI algorithms, real-time data processing, and integrated systems that communicate across every sector of life. It uses your personal profile, daily schedule, and mood (yes, it's that smart) to optimize every interaction. Here's how it unfolds in practice:

Each morning, your personal AI assistant let's call him "Queuebert" reviews your schedule. Queuebert coordinates with the UQS to book your dry cleaning pickup, arrange your grocery delivery (tier based on your laziness), and subtly nudge you to reschedule that dentist appointment you've been avoiding. The magic happens in real-time, with Queuebert continuously refining your day so efficiently that even your coffee breaks are optimized for maximum caffeine joy.

A Day in the Life with UQS

Let's imagine your typical Tuesday, made frictionless by the Universal Queue System—but with you calling the shots. You wake up to Queuebert gently pinging your phone: "Would you like me to order your usual coffee? It can arrive by drone in 20 minutes." You tap "yes" because, let's be honest, caffeine waits for no one.

By the time you're out of the shower, the drone has landed, and your perfectly sealed cup is waiting on your doorstep, exactly as you approved. As you sip, Queuebert notifies you: "Your groceries are scheduled to arrive within the hour. Confirm or reschedule?" You glance at your calendar on your smartwatch and approve, knowing you'll be home to unpack them.

Queuebert continues to make your day easier but always asks first. "Do you want the oil change technician to come to your driveway at 2 p.m.?" "Shall I proceed with booking your doctor's appointment for 1:15 p.m.?" Every task comes with a prompt for your approval, giving you the freedom to adjust or opt out.

By the end of the day, you've saved nearly an hour of cumulative time. No waiting in lines. No wasted commutes. Little nudges of convenience that keep your day on track, ensuring you're in charge and not merely along for the AI-powered ride.

Universal Access: No One Left Behind

Unlike most tech innovations, this one actually has a basic free tier. Think of it like roads, libraries, or tap water—a public utility accessible to everyone.

Of course, premium features exist (because, let's be real, someone always wants VIP treatment). Faster scheduling, priority access, AI-driven concierge services—if there's a way to pay to skip the line, you can bet someone will monetize it.

So, yeah, you could call it "Queue Plus Ultra"—because who are we trying to kid? But at least the core functions—scheduling, queue coordination, and optimization—are available to all. No hidden fees, no "pay-to-play" tax on simply existing. It's as fair as tech gets... which, let's be honest, isn't saying much.

Think of the free tier as a public utility, like electricity or clean water (in theory). Thanks to government backing, this level serves everyone equally, from billionaires booking space vacations to your neighbor desperately trying to get through airport security with a yoga mat. Pure fairness, funded by the fine folks who brought you roads and libraries. Governments recognize that at a basic level reducing inefficiencies at a societal level leads to economic gains, environmental benefits, and happier citizens. Imagine a world where your local taxes support a system that saves you hours every week. Suddenly, "public spending" doesn't sound so bad when it's giving you back time to binge-watch your favorite series guilt-free.

The beauty of the UQS is its versatility. It's not just about skipping lines—it's about skipping *life's inefficiencies*.

Grocery Shopping: Three Tiers of Bliss

Forget aisles. Forget checkout lines. Forget that awkward moment when the self-checkout yells "Unexpected item in bagging area!"

At the economy tier (still free, mind you), you drive to a pickup point, and a cheerful UQS bot loads your groceries into your car. The standard tier? Your groceries arrive by drone, delicately landing on your doorstep like a gift from the gods. And for those opting for the premium tier, your fridge is restocked within the hour, with produce lovingly arranged by a robot programmed to understand your color-coding obsession. Queuebert handles the entire process, notifying you of updates and ensuring your preferences are met. Hate cilantro? Queuebert remembers.

Healthcare: Goodbye, Waiting Rooms

Doctors' offices, once a temple of sad outdated magazines, have been revolutionized. The UQS ensures you arrive almost exactly when your doctor is ready, eliminating awkward small talk with other patients. Minor health issues? Queuebert schedules a telehealth consultation, and medication arrives by drone before you can even sneeze. It's like having a personal health concierge who knows you'd rather binge-watch a series than sit under fluorescent lights.

Concerts and Events: Free to Roam

Virtual queuing for sold-out events is the new norm. Waiting in line? That's for people stuck in 2025. The UQS pings you when it's your turn to enter, leaving you free to grab a snack or overanalyze your outfit. Queuebert can even trade your spot with someone else's if it knows you'd rather linger over your nachos. And for the truly strategic, queue-trading lets you swap spots—because why shouldn't your friend's flexible schedule get you front-row seats?

Travel: A New Kind of Jet Set

Travel is seamless. Airports, train stations, and highways—all optimized by the UQS. Security checkpoints are allocated dynamically, ensuring no lane feels like an endurance test designed by Kafka. Missed connections become a thing of the past as predictive algorithms reroute you before chaos strikes. Your personal AI assistant works hand-in-hand with the UQS, rebooking flights or securing upgrades while you sit back and relax.

Everyday Errands: Delegate and Dominate

Why waste time on dry cleaning or oil changes? Queuebert takes care of it all. It books your errands during the least disruptive time slots, arranges for pickups and deliveries, and even texts you when it's done. You're left to focus on what really matters—like trying out that goat yoga class.

The Hidden Risks: Who's Really in Control?

At first glance, the UQS seems like a techno-utopian dream. But before we get too comfortable with the idea of an AI scheduling our lives down to the perfect latte drop-off time, it's worth asking: What are we giving up?

Yuval Noah Harari, in his book *Nexus*, explores how automation, AI, and predictive algorithms are reshaping human agency. His concern? The more we offload decision-making to machines, the less we actively engage with the world.

This isn't just a theoretical worry—it's already happening. Navigation apps dictate our routes. Recommendation algorithms curate our entertainment. If an AI is managing your schedule, nudging your preferences, and subtly influencing where you go, when, and why—who's actually in charge?

What happens when:

- Your AI decides you "prefer" one grocery store over another—because it's easier for the system, not for you?
- Your doctor's appointment is scheduled at an inconvenient location simply because it optimizes the overall network?
- Your personal schedule starts feeling less like a choice and more like a pre-determined path?

The danger isn't just privacy concerns or economic inequities—though those are real. The deeper issue is autonomy. Are we making choices, or are choices being made for us?

Harari warns that AI-driven convenience could lead to a world where we surrender too much control. If a machine anticipates our needs, smooths out every inefficiency, and subtly guides our daily lives, will we even notice when we stop making real decisions?

"The moment we become passive passengers in our own existence, we are no longer fully human."

This isn't an argument against efficiency—it's a caution about dependence. AI-driven systems should empower us, not override us. The UQS has the potential to revolutionize waiting for the better, but only if we remain conscious of who's in control.

Queue Management: The Future is Already Here

Bottom line? The future is already moving in Queuebert's direction.

Several companies are pioneering AI-driven queue management today, reshaping how we wait:

- QLess allows users to virtually queue for everything from doctor's visits to theme park rides.
- Accesso offers a similar system for major attractions, letting guests schedule ride times instead of physically standing in line.
- Wavetec has brought its queue-busting magic to banks and retail stores, making waiting so invisible you'd think it entered the witness protection program.

These early innovations are just the beginning. The Universal Queue System might still be a future vision, but the groundwork is already being laid. The age of endless waiting is on its way out. The real question is: how much of our decision-making are we willing to hand over in exchange for efficiency?

First, Read the Fine Print: Risks to Consider

Before rushing to fully implement a Universal Queue System, it's worth pausing to consider the potential risks lurking beneath its polished surface. Because let's be honest, no brilliant concept is complete without a few wrinkles that need ironing—or at least a good attempt with a steamer.

Data Privacy Concerns

The UQS would require unprecedented amounts of personal data to operate. Your preferences, habits, and even your physical movements would need to be logged and processed. While it sounds convenient, it also opens the door to misuse. Imagine Queuebert accidentally sharing your aversion to kale with your fitness app—"Shame notification: Did you know kale boosts longevity?"

Over-Reliance on Technology

What happens if the system crashes? A global queue system failure could lead to chaos: drones circling endlessly, grocery pickups piling up, and millions of people stranded at airports. It's like taking away electricity in a world that's forgotten how to light a candle.

Inequities in Access

Will universal access truly remain universal? If governments start slashing budgets, will features like drone delivery or real-time optimization become premium services? The risk of economic disparity creeping into this egalitarian vision shouldn't be underestimated.

Cultural Resistance

In certain parts of the world, standing in line is less about getting served and more about making friends. Streamlining it risks turning warm, communal griping into cold, impersonal efficiency.

So, while the Universal Queue System might sound like a fantasy, its seeds are already sprouting in the real world. The battle against waiting is heating up, with cities and companies chipping away at the queues of yesteryear. Soon, your AI assistant might whisper, "I've moved your dentist appointment to next year—no cavities yet anyway," and hand you a latte.

But remember, progress always comes with a fine print. To truly embrace this future, we must ensure that these systems are equitable, secure, and culturally sensitive—because some things, like our trust and autonomy, should never be put on hold.

Chapter Fourteen

The Future is Now: Cities That Make the Rest of Us Look Bad

"We built this city!" – Starship, *We Built This City*
(*...on data analytics, AI traffic lights, and the crushing realization that your city still hasn't even fixed that one pothole.*)

The world's smartest cities have basically hacked urban life—turning commutes into a breeze, making garbage disposal a source of clean energy, and proving that public transit can be efficient, reliable, and—dare I say—not make you hate everything?

In the land where common sense dies (not naming names, but let's just say certain major American metropolises know who they are) are still passionately debating whether bike lanes are a communist conspiracy or if filling potholes should come before funding yet another stadium nobody asked for.

But smart cities aren't just about slapping some AI onto traffic lights and calling it progress. They're about creating spaces that are greener, saner, and way less infuriating. They eliminate unnecessary waiting—the silent, sanity-eroding tax we all pay when we're stuck in traffic, lingering in endless government lines, or refreshing a train schedule that still doesn't make sense. The future isn't about moving faster—it's about wasting less time.

So what happens when a city gets it right? Time for a global tour of the overachievers—the places where innovation meets urban planning, and where tax dollars actually seem to buy things people want, instead of disappearing into a bureaucratic black hole. Strap in, cupcake—it's time to see what happens when cities actually work on purpose.

Zurich, Switzerland: The City That Runs Like a Swiss Watch

Zurich is what happens when a city takes efficiency personally. While the rest of the world is still trying to figure out how to get their buses to show up on time, Zurich is ranked the #1 Smart City in the world in 2024, according to the IMD Smart Cities Index. This is a place where public transport arrives with the precision of an atomic clock, recycling is practically a competitive sport, and even the river water is so clean, you could probably bottle it and sell it as artisanal Swiss hydration (now with ethically sourced free-range fish poop!).

Public Transit So Perfect, It's Almost Suspicious

Zurich's public transportation system is so punctual, locals claim you can set your watch by the trams. Buses? They arrive precisely on schedule, every time. Trains? Forget delays—if your train is late, it's either rip in the space-time continuum or some other rare cosmic disturbance. The city runs on a highly sophisticated AI-driven public transport synchronization system, which ensures that everything from trams to ferries runs seamlessly—so much so that waiting is practically a foreign concept here.

According to the 2024 Zurich Smart Mobility Report, over 80% of Zurich residents rely on public transit daily because it's that f-ing good. The city has eliminated unnecessary waiting times by perfecting predictive analytics, meaning your tram shows up exactly when you need it, not a second before or after. Elsewhere, ride-sharing and app-based bike and scooter rentals are so flawlessly integrated that even borrowing a two-wheeler feels like a five-star service.

Where Trash Becomes Treasure (Literally)

Zurich doesn't just dispose of waste—it turns it into energy. The city's waste-to-energy plants power thousands of homes, meaning even your leftover cheese fondue contributes to keeping the lights on. The recycling system is so precise, residents get emotionally invested in sorting plastics, paper, and bio-waste correctly—because in Zurich, getting recycling wrong is practically a social crime.

A Green Paradise With Tech to Match

Zurich isn't just smart—it's obnoxiously sustainable in the best way possible. The entire city center is car-free, with walkable streets and AI-controlled green waves for cyclists (meaning if you're on a bike, you'll never hit a red light—ever). The city has also invested in green rooftops, vertical gardens, and energy-efficient buildings that self-regulate temperature, proving that even Zurich's architecture has a better work ethic than most humans.

According to the 2024 European Green Cities Index, Zurich ranks #1 in urban sustainability, cutting emissions by over 50% since 2010, and running entire districts on renewable energy. If the world ends, Zurich will probably still have a backup power supply, clean drinking water, and an efficient tram system—just in case.

The Bottom Line: A City That's Smarter Than Your Smartwatch

Zurich is leading the smart city revolution—and it's lapped the competition, taken a victory lap, and still arrived on time. With flawless public transport, sustainability on overdrive, and an urban design that eliminates inefficiencies before they exist, Zurich is proof that a city can be both futuristic and effortlessly livable. If there were an Olympic event for urban planning, Zurich would take gold—and then recycle the medal into an energy-efficient power grid.

Singapore: The City That Plans for Tomorrow Yesterday

Singapore builds for the future like it's already been there in a time machine, taken notes, and come back with a five-step improvement plan. This is a city where efficiency is borderline obsessive, greenery covers literally every surface possible, and public transportation runs with the precision of a Swiss watch (made in Zurich perhaps?) strapped to an overachiever's wrist. If cities had report cards, Singapore would be that student who not only aces the test but also corrects the teacher's mistakes.

Public Transport So Reliable, You Could Bet Your Lunch On It

Singapore's Mass Rapid Transit (MRT) system is the kind of thing most cities write wistful poetry about. It's fast, clean, and so punctual that locals don't even check the schedule anymore. A 2023 Global Transit Report ranked the MRT among the top 3 most reliable metro systems in the world, with an on-time performance of over 99.5%. That means if your train is late, you're either in an alternate quantum universe or it's your fault for existing outside the laws of Singaporean efficiency.

Buses? Also automated, shockingly smooth, and run so frequently that you'll start thinking they operate on telepathy. The government has invested heavily in AI-driven transport logistics that dynamically adjust schedules based on real-time commuter demand, cutting wait times to mere seconds in high-traffic areas.

And because walking in Singapore shouldn't feel like training for an ultramarathon, the city has a network of air-conditioned walkways and underground pedestrian tunnels, so you can get where you're going without sweating through your carefully chosen outfit.

Green Enough to Make Other Cities Jealous

Most cities struggle to maintain a few trees; Singapore built an entire forest into its skyline. The city is practically a botanical garden in disguise, with vertical gardens draped over skyscrapers, rooftop farms growing actual produce, and solar-powered supertrees that wouldn't look out of place in a sci-fi movie.

The government isn't planting greenery for show—it's integrating nature into urban planning. According to a 2023 Sustainable Cities Index, Singapore ranks #1 in the world for urban green space per capita, proving that you can build a dense metropolis *and* make it feel like a jungle retreat at the same time.

The city's commitment to sustainability doesn't stop at aesthetics. Waste incineration generates power, seawater is desalinated for drinking, and even the air-conditioning is centrally optimized to reduce energy waste. The entire city is engineered to be both smart and eco-friendly—kind of like if your laptop and a rainforest had a baby.

Technology That Actually Works (And Won't Make You Cry)

Singapore runs on AI-powered everything, but unlike in other cities where "smart tech" just means *Wi-Fi that never works*, here, it actually does its job. The entire city operates under a predictive analytics system, meaning everything from traffic lights to emergency response is optimized before problems even arise.

Even Changi Airport—repeatedly voted the best airport in the world—is so luxurious and efficient that layovers here feel like vacations. There's a butterfly garden, a waterfall, and a movie theater. You can literally miss your flight and still have the best day of your life.

The Bottom Line: The City of the Future That's Already Here

Singapore isn't trying to be a smart city—it's the one all the others copy off of. With flawless public transport, AI-run infrastructure, and a green urban paradise that other cities can only dream about, it proves that urban living doesn't have to be stressful, wasteful, or just plain annoying. While other places struggle to keep the buses running, Singapore is out here rewriting the rulebook on what a city can be.

Copenhagen, Denmark: Bikes, Brains, and Brunch

Copenhagen is the Beyoncé of smart cities: effortlessly cool, green, and always ahead of the curve. It's a cyclist's paradise, with more bikes than people and highways built specifically for them.

Waiting in traffic? Not here—bikes glide through the city faster than cars in most places, thanks to dedicated lanes and smart traffic lights that prioritize cyclists. I already gushed about this in an earlier chapter because, frankly, I can't get enough. The 'green wave' system times lights so cyclists can ride through the city without ever stopping, and here we are again, fanboying like an American who just discovered espresso in Italy. According to the Danish Road Directorate, this system has improved cycling speeds by 17% and reduced travel times by 10 minutes per day for regular commuters.

The city's renewable energy systems power almost everything, and surplus energy is exported to neighboring countries. The harbor is clean enough to swim in—yes, they've turned a major urban port into a swimming pool, complete with diving platforms.

Copenhagen has smart trash cans in public spaces that notify waste collectors when they're full—because instead of emptying half-full bins on a rigid schedule, the city figured it's smarter to collect garbage *when it actually needs collecting*. Less wasted effort, fewer overflowing bins, and probably a few confused pigeons wondering where their buffet went. As if that weren't smart enough, the city's streetlights dim when no one's around, conserving energy while still managing to look hygge as hell.

Oslo, Norway: Where Oil Money Went Green

Oslo has achieved what seemed impossible: taking an oil-rich economy and turning it into one of the greenest, most efficient cities on the planet. While other capitals are still arguing about banning plastic straws, Oslo is out here running an entire public transport network on renewable energy and making cars almost entirely unnecessary. The city isn't just smart—it's strategically dismantling the need for waiting, waste, and pollution.

But here's the plot twist: this entire green revolution was bankrolled by oil money.

In the late 1960s, Norway struck black gold in the North Sea, and by the 1970s, the country was swimming in petroleum profits. Unlike other resource-rich nations that treated oil money like an all-you-can-spend buffet, Norway played the long game. In 1990, it set up the Government Pension Fund Global (a.k.a. the Oil Fund), a sovereign wealth fund that now holds over $1.4 trillion, making it the largest of its kind in the world.

This isn't a stash of cash gathering cobwebs—it's strategically invested in ethical, sustainable industries, making sure Norway's oil wealth builds a future, not just a fleeting fortune. Oslo took that oil money, did a dramatic mic drop, and sprinted full speed into the future—probably on an electric bike. The capital has aggressively distanced itself from fossil fuels and poured its wealth into renewable energy, electric transport, and car-free urban planning.

A Car-Free Utopia (Almost)

Oslo has been on a mission to remove cars from its city center, replacing them with electric buses, trams, and bike lanes wider than some highways. And it's working. According to a 2023 Norwegian Urban Mobility Report, car traffic in the downtown core has dropped by 35% in the past five years, making it one of the most pedestrian-friendly capitals in Europe.

If you do need a car, odds are it's electric. Oslo boasts the highest percentage of EV ownership per capita in the world—a whopping 80% of new cars sold in 2023 were electric, thanks to aggressive government incentives and an infrastructure that makes charging stations as common as coffee shops (which, in Norway, is saying something).

Public Transit: So Good You Forget Cars Exist

Hopping on a tram in Oslo feels less like public transit and more like a victory lap for the planet—zero emissions, zero guilt, and zero chance of your seat being mysteriously sticky.

And if you think waiting for a bus is inevitable, think again. The city's AI-powered transport system dynamically adjusts schedules based on real-time demand, meaning you'll rarely stand at a stop wondering if you should've just walked. According to 2023 data from Ruter, Oslo's public transit authority, average wait times have dropped by 40% since AI implementation, making "just-missed-the-tram" rage a thing of the past.

Smart Infrastructure That Actually Works

Oslo doesn't just do sustainability—it makes it wildly convenient. Smart pedestrian crossings detect your walking speed and adjust signals accordingly, because apparently, Norwegians refuse to be rushed *or* delayed. Buildings are heated with excess energy from garbage incineration plants, and entire neighborhoods run on district heating systems that recycle energy back into the grid.

Even the city's libraries have gone high-tech, with AI-driven digital lending systems that recommend books based on your previous checkouts. While it's not quite at the level of scanning your face to decide whether you need a self-help book, it's getting there.

The Bottom Line: A City That Runs Like a Dream

Ironically, the same oil money that made Norway rich is now funding the transition away from fossil fuels. Oslo is proof that an oil-based economy doesn't have to mean an oil-dependent future—and that with the right planning, even a city built on petroleum can become one of the greenest in the world, proving that a fossil fuel-based economy doesn't mean a fossilized city. With its car-free push, AI-powered transit, and green energy dominance, it's among the most sustainable cities in the world—and one of the most efficient. If the rest of the world wants to know what a smart urban future looks like, they might want to start paying attention to Norway.

Dubai, United Arab Emirates: The Jetsons, but Make It Real

Dubai doesn't do small; it does spectacle. If there's a way to make something bigger, taller, or more futuristic, Dubai has already done it—and then added a laser show. While most cities struggle to synchronize their traffic lights, Dubai is busy testing autonomous flying taxis, zipping between solar-powered skyscrapers like a sci-fi fever dream. According to a 2023 UAE Smart Transit Report, Dubai aims to have 25% of all transport autonomous by 2030, proving once again that while other cities debate bike lanes, Dubai is out here building a literal Jetsons reality.

AI-Powered Everything (Yes, Even the Cops)

Dubai's public transport system is a marvel of efficiency, where AI doesn't just assist—it runs the whole show. The driverless Dubai Metro is already one of the longest fully automated metro networks in the world, and AI-powered scheduling eliminates delays by predicting and preventing bottlenecks before they occur. Because no futuristic city is complete without robo-cop, Dubai's police force includes actual robot officers—which, if nothing else, means you might one day get a speeding ticket from a polite android with perfect posture.

And if that weren't futuristic enough, drones deliver groceries, legal documents, and even medical supplies, proving that in Dubai, waiting is for other people.

A Walkable Oasis in the Desert

Despite its love for supercars and skyscrapers, Dubai is shockingly pedestrian-friendly. The city center is packed with shaded promenades, air-conditioned bus stops, and open-air malls designed to keep pedestrians comfortable—even when the desert sun is doing its best impression of an oven. The government is also doubling down on green transport, with a huge expansion of electric bus networks and dedicated cycling paths (because yes, even in Dubai, biking is becoming a thing).

Smart City, Smarter Palm Trees

Even the city's palm trees aren't just decorative—they double as Wi-Fi hotspots and solar energy hubs. Because in Dubai, a tree isn't just a tree; it's a data center with leaves. The city has also rolled out smart benches that charge your phone, because if you're going to sit, you might as well sit in a tech-powered future.

No surprise here, not everything is seamless—sometimes the robots get a little too enthusiastic. One resident reported being fined by a robo-cop for jaywalking while still on the sidewalk. In Dubai, even your law enforcement is ahead of schedule.

The Bottom Line: A City From the Future (But It's Real)

Dubai isn't just aiming to be a smart city—it's building a blueprint for sci-fi urbanism in real time. From AI-powered transit to solar-fueled skyscrapers and Wi-Fi-enabled landscaping, this is a city that doesn't wait for the future—it invents it.

Chengdu, China: The Quiet Giant That's Smarter Than Your Average Megacity

Chengdu (pop. 20 million) might not shout about its brilliance, but it quietly gets everything right. While some megacities battle daily logistical nightmares, Chengdu has mastered the art of effortless urban living—without making a big fuss about it. You won't hear dramatic proclamations about being a futuristic metropolis, but if smart cities had a zen master, it would be Chengdu.

In most cities, moving 20 million people a day would mean gridlock and stress. In Chengdu, it means clean, punctual public transit and streets designed for both speed and strolls. AI-powered scheduling keeps everything running efficiently, making it one of the most livable megacities on the planet. According to a 2023 Chengdu Urban Mobility Report, bus and metro punctuality rates exceed 98%, and if your ride is late, you should probably assume time itself has broken.

It's not only about efficiency—it's about ease. The entire city's transit system is cashless and app-based, meaning you can glide through metro stations, rent a bike, and even pay for a cab without ever reaching for your wallet. Public transport is so well-integrated that a multi-modal trip (bus, metro, shared bike) rarely takes longer than a single-car ride—and unlike sitting in traffic, it won't raise your blood pressure.

Green, Gorgeous, and Air-Purifying

Chengdu has fully embraced sustainable urban design without making it feel like a marketing gimmick. The city's adaptive streetlights adjust to weather and traffic conditions, conserving energy while improving safety. Buildings aren't just energy-efficient—they're living structures, covered in plant life that naturally filters air pollution. According to the 2023 China Green Cities Index, Chengdu has one of the lowest air pollution levels among major Chinese cities—no small feat for a metropolis this size.

But Chengdu's biggest flex? Urban farming zones. The city has pioneered a model where residents can grow their own vegetables on shared rooftop gardens, effectively turning unused urban spaces into productive greenhouses. This isn't just a cute trend—it's a citywide push toward local food security and sustainability, reducing the carbon footprint of food transport while giving locals access to fresh, hyper-local produce.

Pedestrian Paradise & AI-Powered Dining

While many cities dream about walkability, Chengdu actually delivers. The city center is car-free, with wide boulevards shaded by trees, park-lined pedestrian streets, and hidden alleyways filled with vibrant markets. The result? A calm, green atmosphere where walking feels like a luxury rather than a necessity.

The Bottom Line: The Future is Chill

While other smart cities focus on speed, Chengdu focuses on flow—a city designed to work so seamlessly that you barely notice how efficient it is. From its hyper-connected public transit to its green urban design and AI-enhanced culinary scene, Chengdu proves that a high-tech city doesn't have to feel high-stress. It's futuristic, it's sustainable, and—most impressively—it manages to be all of that without losing its soul.

Ljubljana Slovenia: The Green Jewel of Europe

Ljubljana may be small, but it punches well above its weight. This European Green Capital is so committed to eco-friendliness that it's practically allergic to pollution. The entire city center is car-free, with electric shuttles known as Kavalirs (which translates to "Gentlemen") quietly ferrying people from point A to point B. Instead of honking and traffic jams, Ljubljana's core is now a pedestrian's dream filled with lively cafés, street musicians, and public art.

If you're wondering whether banning cars makes a difference, the answer is a resounding yes. Since pedestrianization, Ljubljana has seen a 70% reduction in motor traffic in the city center, and air quality has improved significantly, according to a 2022 EU Urban Sustainability Report.

Ljubljana's waste management system is so efficient that they've been named Europe's Green Capital multiple times. The city boasts one of the highest waste separation and recycling rates in Europe, with over 68% of its waste being recycled. Their underground, vacuum-powered waste collection system eliminates the need for noisy, diesel-powered garbage trucks, while an AI-powered tracking system ensures waste bins are only emptied when full, reducing unnecessary collections by 30%, as per the Slovenian Environmental Agency.

Waiting for a shuttle? Nearly non-existent. Ljubljana's real-time transport app doesn't just tell you when the next bus is coming—it makes sure you're never left staring into the abyss of public transit uncertainty. The city's buses are basically mind readers, using a smart scheduling system that adjusts to traffic and demand, so you're not left wondering if you should've just walked.

And then, there's the water. Ljubljana's water system is entirely natural—no chemicals, just pure, delicious H2O straight from underground springs. Residents say that their tap water is better than any bottled brand, and frankly, they're right. Ljubljana has also refused to privatize its water supply, ensuring it remains a public good for all residents.

Oh, and before you embarrass yourself at dinner trying to say the name, it's pronounced 'lyoob-lyah-nah.' Don't worry, you're not alone—half of its visitors take one look at the spelling and assume it's an elaborate brain teaser. But once you get past that, you'll realize Ljubljana isn't only easy on the tongue—it's easy on the planet, too.

Ljubljana's commitment to sustainability is so hardcore, even its public spaces are in on the action.

The city's parks run on solar power, and their Christmas lights are so energy-efficient that Santa himself would approve. It's the kind of place where you instinctively sort your recyclables at a picnic and feel guilty for even thinking about using a plastic straw.

And because Ljubljana doesn't just want to be green—it wants to look good while doing it—the city has fully embraced the green architecture movement. Rooftop gardens, solar-powered streetlights, and vertical green walls are everywhere, creating a city that looks like a living, breathing eco-experiment—and it's working.

Riga Latvia: The Tech Whisperer

Riga is what happens when a medieval city meets a tech startup and they decide to raise a future together. Walking through its cobblestone streets, you half expect to see knights in shining armor—but instead, you get biogas-powered buses, AI-driven public transport, and a city that practically runs on automation.

Public transport here doesn't mess around—it anticipates your next move like a mind-reading fortune teller. Riga's AI-powered transit system dynamically adjusts routes and schedules in real-time based on commuter demand. So instead of staring at a bus timetable and wondering whether you should just start walking, you get a bus that actually arrives when and where you need it. According to a 2023 Smart Mobility Study, Riga's AI-driven scheduling has reduced average wait times by 35% and cut down on unnecessary fuel consumption by 20%, making the city both more efficient and greener.

Oh, you thought that was it? Hell no—we're just getting warmed up. Riga's historic buildings have been secretly upgraded with smart tech, like a grandma who suddenly knows how to use TikTok. Sensors for energy efficiency are tucked away so well, you'd never guess the place was running on cutting-edge tech instead of candlelight. Want to charge your phone while admiring centuries-old architecture? Go for it—Riga's got you covered. The city's smart benches not only let you juice up your battery, but also provide free Wi-Fi, because even Instagramming your perfect European vacation requires cutting-edge infrastructure.

The city has also pioneered contactless everything—from digital ID systems that let you access municipal services without paperwork to an AI-powered waste collection system that ensures garbage is picked up only when needed, eliminating inefficient collection routes. Waste bins are embedded with sensors that notify collectors when they're full, meaning no more overflowing trash or unnecessary fuel use from trucks emptying half-full bins. This has cut waste-related traffic by

25%, according to the Latvian Environmental Research Institute.

And because Riga knows that the secret to a happy city is keeping relationships intact, they've installed 24/7 flower vending machines all over town. Forgot an anniversary? Riga's got your back. Need an emergency apology bouquet? The city has you covered. Latvia might be a small country, but its capital is proving that smart cities aren't just about efficiency—they're about making life smoother, funnier, and infinitely more convenient.

Canberra, Australia: A Capital Idea

Canberra doesn't get the same hype as Sydney or Melbourne, but it's proving that smaller cities can go toe-to-toe with the best in innovation. Often dismissed as just "the place where Australia's politicians argue," Canberra has been busy transforming itself into a sustainability powerhouse.

First up: solar energy domination. Canberra is well on its way to becoming Australia's first 100% renewable-powered city, with large-scale solar and wind farms already generating most of its electricity. According to a 2023 Australian Renewable Energy Agency report, the city has reduced its carbon footprint by over 40% since 2010, all while keeping the lights on and the Wi-Fi strong.

Public transport here is also ahead of the curve. The Canberra Light Rail, introduced in 2019, is fully electric, zero-emission, and surprisingly efficient—because apparently, Canberra didn't get the memo that public transit is supposed to be a test of patience. Canberra's bus system follows suit, with an increasing number of electric buses added each year. And thanks to real-time tracking apps, residents no longer have to wonder whether they'll be stranded at a bus stop indefinitely.

Speaking of traffic, Canberra is often promoted as a "20-minute city," suggesting that daily commutes are typically short and free from major congestion. Want to build a 20-minute city? Take one part intelligent traffic management, a generous helping of efficient public transit, and just a pinch of walkability (because let's be real, nobody wants to *actually* sprint to a bus stop). Canberra seems to have perfected the recipe, with its Sydney Coordinated Adaptive Traffic System (SCATS) keeping cars moving, a bus network designed to get people where they need to go without feeling like they've boarded a cross-country expedition, and a city layout that actually encourages people to get out of their cars once in a while.

According to 2024 ACT Government data, this approach has helped keep congestion low and commute times short—so while other cities are debating whether they should maybe *consider* bike lanes, Canberra's already out here making urban planning look effortless. The result? A place where you can get across town faster than it takes some people to find their car keys.

Canberra's commitment to green space is nothing short of heroic. According to the ACT State of the Environment Report, conservation areas protect 60% of the total ACT area, encompassing parks, nature reserves, and green zones—because apparently, this city took 'leave no trace' as a personal challenge. The city is actively working toward increasing this percentage, proving that you can have a capital city that's both functional and refreshingly breathable. It's the kind of place where you can actually take a deep breath without wondering what just entered your lungs. If cities had lungs, Canberra's would be doing yoga and drinking a kale smoothie.

The city's urban design prioritizes pedestrian and cyclist infrastructure, with dedicated bike paths that wind through nature rather than forcing commuters to dodge traffic.

Speaking of things that rarely get praised, government efficiency is actually a thing here. Canberra has been digitizing municipal services at an impressive pace, allowing residents to handle everything from tax filings to building permits online, without needing to suffer through long queues or bureaucratic limbo. An AI-powered city portal now streamlines most government interactions, cutting processing times by 35% according to a 2023 Australian Smart Cities Index.

So while it may not have the glitz of Sydney's harbor or Melbourne's coffee scene, Canberra is proving that smart city innovation doesn't have to come with a side of chaos. With renewable energy, intelligent transport, and digital government services making life easier, Canberra is a quiet overachiever that's paving the way for a greener, more efficient future.

Geneva, Switzerland: Diplomacy Meets Data

Geneva may be best known for its role in global diplomacy, but it's also a smart city powerhouse. While politicians are busy solving global conflicts, Geneva is quietly optimizing urban life with ruthless Swiss efficiency—and let's be honest, it probably has a hidden James Bond villain lair somewhere under the UN complex.

In Geneva, hopping between trams, buses, and boats is seamless. A real-time traffic monitoring system constantly fine-tunes routes and schedules, keeping delays to a minimum. A 2023 European Smart Transit Report ranked Geneva's transit system among the top 5 most efficient in Europe, with commuters spending 20% less time in transit than in comparable cities. And let's not forget the electric ferries—yes, you can literally commute across Lake Geneva while sipping an espresso, enjoying a mountain view, and wondering why your own city can't get it together.

The city has also embraced smart technology, with sensors that monitor air quality and adaptive traffic systems that keep the city moving smoothly. This has led to a 15% drop in CO_2 levels in high-traffic areas, according to the European Environmental Agency. Geneva's car-free zones are full of cobblestones, flowers, and postcard-perfect cafés, making walking around feel like stepping into a meticulously curated Instagram feed.

Geneva is also a global leader in sustainability. The city's ambitious climate strategy aims for carbon neutrality by 2050, with 80% of municipal energy already coming from renewable sources, as per a 2023 Swiss Energy Report. Geneva's underground heating and cooling system reduces energy consumption by 30%, a marvel of urban design that makes even the United Nations complex one of the greenest office buildings on the planet—which is fitting, considering how much hot air gets generated there daily.

And since Geneva is the diplomatic capital of the world, it takes digital privacy and smart governance incredibly seriously. The city's AI-driven municipal platform allows residents to pay taxes, renew licenses, and schedule government services without having to stand in a single line—which, frankly, might be Geneva's most impressive feat yet. A 2023 Swiss Digital Governance Study reported that over 85% of Geneva's residents handle administrative tasks online, slashing paperwork processing times by 40% and making bureaucratic nightmares a thing of the past. (No more losing half your life to a waiting room filled with flickering fluorescent lights—take notes, DMV.)

Even Geneva's urban design is optimized for efficiency. Parks, sidewalks, and green spaces are designed with pedestrian-first planning, making it easier to walk, cycle, or just exist without feeling like you're constantly dodging cars. It's no surprise that Geneva consistently ranks among the most livable cities in the world, according to the 2023 Mercer Quality of Living Index—turns out, when a city invests in sustainability, transport, and digital services, people actually enjoy living there. Who knew?

In short, Geneva may be famous for diplomacy, but its real superpower is turning city life into a stress-free, hyper-efficient dream. Other cities, take notes—this is how you build a metropolis that actually works.

London, United Kingdom: Big Ben Meets Big Data

London may be old enough to have invented queues, but its transport system is powered by AI so smart it feels like it's reading your mind—or at least your train schedule. While tourists struggle to figure out which way to stand on an escalator (it's the right, and yes, people *will* judge you if you get it wrong), locals benefit from a public transport network that's constantly evolving to keep up with one of the busiest cities on Earth.

One of London's biggest wins? The congestion charge, which has reduced traffic in the city center by 30% since its introduction, according to a 2023 Transport for London (TfL) report. Not only has this made the city more walkable, but it's also cut emissions and made breathing in the middle of Oxford Circus feel *slightly* less like inhaling a car exhaust. London has also rolled out an Ultra Low Emission Zone (ULEZ), which forces polluting vehicles to pay a hefty fee—because nothing motivates people to ditch their gas-guzzlers like a hit to their wallets. And yet, someone in a Range Rover will still insist on squeezing down a side street clearly designed for a horse and cart.

And when it comes to public transit, London isn't playing around. The Elizabeth Line, completed in 2022, has slashed travel times across the city, reducing congestion on other Tube lines and making the daily commute feel *almost* tolerable. AI-powered train scheduling systems have improved efficiency by 20%, keeping delays at a minimum (or at least making them slightly less rage-inducing). And in another win for people who hate surprises, real-time bus tracking ensures you know *exactly* when to expect the next double-decker—no more squinting into the distance and wondering if you should just start walking. (You should, though. It's London. You'll probably get there faster, and it's a great excuse for a roll en route.)

Beyond transport, London is going vertical—literally. Urban farming has exploded across the city, with rooftop gardens, vertical farms, and underground hydroponic systems turning unused spaces into food production hubs. According to a 2023 London Sustainable Cities Report, these initiatives have increased locally grown food output by 35%, reducing reliance on imports and cutting down food miles. So while the weather might still be legally required to be unpredictable, at least the city's green spaces are thriving—both on the ground and in the sky. (Because if you can't predict the sun, you might as well guarantee fresh basil.)

And speaking of indoors, London's advancements in smart building technology are ensuring that while it may be cold and rainy outside, inside remains perfectly cozy. AI-driven heating and cooling systems adjust to occupancy patterns, reducing energy waste and cutting heating costs by 25% in commercial buildings, according to the UK Green Building Council. Demonstrating that old-world charm and modern efficiency can actually get along, a growing number of beloved historic buildings are being retrofitted with smart energy solutions—showing that you can preserve history and stay warm without resorting to wearing six layers and clutching a cup of tea for dear life.

London might be steeped in history, but it's also sprinting into the future with a mix of AI, sustainability, and good old-fashioned efficiency. The city proves that you can have Victorian architecture, double-decker buses, and cutting-edge tech all in one place—just don't expect the weather to keep up. And yes, your train will still get mysteriously delayed the moment you're running late, but some British traditions (like complaining about said delays) are simply too sacred to disrupt. Just make sure you've got an emergency stash of biscuits—you never know when the next minor inconvenience might require one.

Helsinki, Finland: Where Smart Tech Meets Arctic Chill

Helsinki is a shining example of what happens when innovation meets Nordic practicality—where urban planning is as efficient as its citizens' ability to queue politely. This city doesn't just embrace the future; it engineers it to withstand subzero temperatures and the kind of darkness that would make even a London winter look cheerful.

Let's start with public transportation, because Helsinki isn't about making you wait in the cold. The city has pioneered autonomous buses, meaning your ride arrives with robotic precision, no disgruntled driver required. Its Mobility as a Service (MaaS) app allows residents to plan, book, and pay for their trips across all modes of transport in one seamless experience. Whether you're hopping on a tram, grabbing a city bike, or even calling a ferry, Helsinki's got it covered—no rummaging through pockets for loose euros required. According to a 2023 Finnish Transport Authority report, MaaS adoption has reduced single-passenger car trips by 22%, easing congestion and keeping the city's streets moving like a well-oiled (renewable) machine.

Speaking of pedestrian-friendly planning, Helsinki's city center is dotted with smart benches that provide Wi-Fi and charge your phone—perfect for when the Northern Lights distract you from monitoring your battery life. These benches also monitor air quality and temperature, because if there's one thing Finland takes seriously, it's knowing exactly how cold it is at all times.

While other cities debate carbon neutrality, Helsinki is busy making it standard practice. The city's renewable-powered energy grid adjusts in real-time to demand, meaning that even in the darkest depths of winter, the lights (and saunas, obviously) stay on. In 2023, the Helsinki Energy Challenge led to a breakthrough in carbon-neutral heating, accelerating the city's plan to phase out coal by 2029—because apparently, Helsinki isn't just ahead of the curve; it's building the curve itself.

And if that wasn't enough to make winter a little less miserable, let's talk about the self-heating streets. Thanks to underground geothermal systems and district heating, Helsinki keeps key walkways and bike paths blissfully ice-free. No salt, no shovels, no slipping on an invisible patch of doom and flailing like a cartoon character. Meanwhile, over in Buffalo, New York, someone is currently digging their car out of a snowdrift and wondering if they should just move to Finland.

Smart city tech in Helsinki doesn't stop at transport and energy—it extends all the way to bureaucracy, and somehow, even that runs smoothly. The city's AI-powered portal lets residents handle everything from renewing licenses to booking public services, cutting out the usual administrative headache. A 2023 European Smart Governance Report ranked Helsinki among the top three cities in Europe for digital public services, proving that when you mix efficiency with Nordic ingenuity, even paperwork becomes painless.

So while Helsinki may be known for long winters, this city is running full speed into the future—with self-driving buses, self-heating streets, and enough smart city tech to make even Silicon Valley jealous. It turns out, you don't need endless sunshine to build a bright future—you just need Finnish efficiency and a really good app.

Honorable Mentions: America's Top 3 (and a Shoutout to Charlotte)

Although no American cities have cracked the top smart cities globally, there are a few bright spots showing potential in the U.S. While Europe and Asia are busy perfecting AI-powered transit systems and carbon-neutral urban utopias, America is still debating whether bike lanes are a secret government plot to steal parking spaces. But hope is not lost—some cities are actually getting things right.

Portland, Oregon: Bikes, Trees, and the Dream of European Transit

Portland's biking culture and urban greenery are top-notch, making it feel like the hipster cousin of Copenhagen—if that cousin also had a crippling public transit dependency. While the city's bus and rail network is still dreaming of a European-level upgrade, it has made impressive strides in sustainable development, renewable energy adoption, and urban walkability. According to the 2023 U.S. Urban Mobility Report, Portland has cut single-passenger car trips by 15% over the past decade—proving that yes, people will actually take the bus if you make it convenient.

Austin, Texas: Solar Panels and Standstill Traffic

Austin has embraced renewable energy with gusto, becoming a national leader in solar power adoption. In fact, the city now sources more than 40% of its energy from renewables, according to a 2023 report by the U.S. Department of Energy. That said, Austin's biggest challenge remains its car-centric design, which makes traffic as much a part of daily life as breakfast tacos and live music. The city is expanding its public transit network, but until Texans collectively agree that public transportation isn't a personal attack on freedom, progress will be slow.

Seattle, Washington: The Cloud Capital's Smart City Push

Seattle, home to tech giants and endless drizzle, is inching closer to becoming a global smart city leader. Seattle, home to tech giants and endless drizzle, is inching closer to becoming a global smart city leader. Seattle is using AI to make commuting slightly less painful—smart traffic lights, a well-connected light rail, and enough eco-friendly buildings to make Mother Nature give a thumbs-up. According to the 2023 Seattle Smart City Index, all that effort has trimmed commute times by 12% since 2015. Progress!

Charlotte, North Carolina: The Unexpected Contender

And now, a well-earned shoutout to Charlotte, because let's be real—I live here, and I'd like to see my city win. Charlotte might not have Portland's biking culture or Seattle's cloud-powered urban planning, but it is quietly making moves in the smart city race. The city's Autonomous Vehicle Initiative is testing driverless public transport, and its data-driven traffic management system is working to ease congestion (which anyone who has been on I-77 at rush hour knows is no small feat).

Charlotte is also pushing toward sustainable urban development, with projects like the Envision Charlotte initiative, which has reduced commercial building energy use by 19% since 2011, according to the U.S. Green Building Council. It may not be topping global smart city rankings just yet, but give it time—this city is on the rise.

Conclusion: A Blueprint for the Future

The smartest cities of today show us what's possible when innovation, sustainability, and a healthy dose of ambition collide. They're not just places to live; they're proof that the future doesn't have to be a flaming dumpster fire. They've taken the annoyances of daily life—traffic, pollution, waiting in endless lines—and systematically eliminated them with technology, walkability, and a refusal to settle for mediocrity.

Because old habits die hard, your city is still convinced that adding one more lane to the highway—yes, the same one that hasn't moved since 2003—will magically solve all its traffic problems. It won't. But sure, go ahead and pave over another neighborhood and see if that helps.

And here's a wild idea: Build cities for people, not cars. I know, crazy talk. Maybe instead of endless suburban sprawl where you have to drive 20 minutes just to buy a loaf of bread, we could try designing places where humans—not SUVs—are the boss. Because last I checked, nobody's dream neighborhood is a five-lane highway with a Walmart parking lot view.

Now, as a North Carolinian, I know a thing or two about big trucks, wide roads, and that deep-seated fear that if you don't have a driveway the size of a football field, you're doing life wrong. But hear me out—what if you could actually walk to your favorite

BBQ joint instead of spending half your life circling for parking? I'm in, how 'bout you?

So while your local government debates whether bike lanes are part of a secret plot to overthrow civilization, remember: the blueprint for a smarter, greener world is already here. The cities leading the way have done the hard work; now it's just a matter of the rest of the world putting down the traffic cones and paying attention.

Chapter Fifteen
The Endless Line

"Anticipation is making me late, is keeping me waiting."—Carly Simon
(Also known as the Waiting National Anthem.)

For all our technological advances, waiting isn't going anywhere. No matter how fast we get, some bottlenecks will always remain—whether imposed by the laws of physics, resource limitations, or the sheer unpredictability of human behavior. Ironically, waiting may be one of life's few constants, right up there with death, taxes, and realizing you forgot an essential grocery item the second you get home.

The Unavoidable Laws of Waiting

Physics doesn't care about our impatience. Even if we bring back supersonic planes, you'd still have to deal with airport security, baggage claims, and the one guy in front of you who suddenly decides to reorganize his carry-on at the last minute. Until we invent teleportation—which, let's be honest, is not happening in our lifetimes—travel will always involve some form of waiting.

Then there's supply and demand. No matter how much we optimize, delays will persist. Crops still have to grow. Factories still need raw materials.

Storms still shut down roads. A world that runs at full speed is also a world prone to traffic jams, shipping backlogs, and holiday-season meltdowns at the post office.

The faster we try to push things, the more we create new bottlenecks elsewhere. It's like widening a faucet to fill a bathtub faster—only to realize the drain is still the same size.

The True Bottleneck: Us

No matter how much we optimize, automate, or throw AI at the problem, we'll never outrun the biggest bottleneck of all: human nature. Procrastination, indecision, and an almost impressive level of obliviousness keep the wheels of inefficiency spinning. No algorithm can override the person holding up the self-checkout line because they *just need a second* to find their coupon. No app can save us from the guy who waits until he's at the counter to start reading the menu like it's a sacred text.

Consider the madness of Black Friday. Every year, retailers roll out *exclusive, limited-time offers*, and every year, people wait until the last possible second—crashing websites, clogging store aisles, and turning the act of purchasing a discounted toaster into a contact sport. This isn't a supply chain problem. It's a *human behavior* problem.

And then there's indecision—the more refined cousin of procrastination. The person standing in line at a coffee shop, staring at the menu like they're decoding ancient hieroglyphics, unable to decide between an oat milk latte and their usual drip coffee, is not a victim of slow service. Multiply that moment of hesitation by hundreds or even thousands of people, and suddenly, you've got systemic delays that no amount of technology can fix.

Even when we create faster options, human resistance keeps the wait alive. Self-checkout lanes were meant to speed things up, but plenty of people still avoid them, preferring to make small talk with the cashier or—worse—struggle with the scanner while an employee eventually has to intervene. While the chosen few zip through TSA PreCheck, that doesn't stop someone in the regular line from forgetting to take their laptop out of their bag and bringing everything to a screeching halt.

Waiting, it turns out, is often a team sport—we sabotage ourselves, and then we blame the game.

The Price of Speed: Who Really Pays for Instant Gratification?

Would a world without waiting be better, or just better for some?

The ability to skip the line is rarely free. Whether it's TSA PreCheck, Disney's Lightning Lane, or a grocery delivery subscription, convenience has a price. The more we engineer waiting out of existence, the more it becomes a tax on those who can't pay their way out. If time is money, then waiting is the cost paid by those who can't afford to bypass it.

Even when technology removes barriers, it often comes with strings attached. Eliminating waiting usually means sacrificing privacy. AI-powered queue management, real-time traffic monitoring, and predictive algorithms all require massive amounts of data. The faster we move, the more we're tracked, analyzed, and nudged toward efficiency.

At first, it feels harmless. Your phone reminds you it's time to reorder your favorite brand of coffee before you even realize you're running low. Your smart fridge notices you're out of almond milk and adds it to the grocery list. But soon, convenience starts making decisions for you. What happens when your insurance company adjusts your premiums based on your snack choices? Or when a fitness app suggests you "rethink" your lifestyle based on how many times you've ordered takeout this month?

The quest to eliminate waiting also takes a toll on the environment. As we explored in an earlier chapter, a world that runs at full speed is an energy-hungry one. Faster shipping means more warehouses, more delivery trucks, and more fuel.

Every second saved often means something lost elsewhere. And when companies prioritize speed over sustainability, the planet pays the price.

So yes, we can make waiting disappear—but at what cost?

A World Without Waiting? Sounds Exhausting

For all our gripes about waiting, maybe it's not the enemy. Maybe, waiting is one of life's undervalued experiences.

There's something to be said for the art of anticipation. Studies show that the build-up to an event—like planning a vacation or counting down to a holiday—can be just as enjoyable as the event itself. Unwrapping a gift is often more thrilling than what's inside. The same applies to experiences. A slow-cooked meal is more satisfying than drive-thru takeout. The joy of reconnecting with an old friend is sweeter because of the time apart. When everything is instant, we lose the satisfaction that comes from waiting for something worthwhile.

Different cultures have long embraced waiting as part of life's rhythm. In Japan, the tea ceremony is an intricate, deliberate process designed to slow people down and cultivate mindfulness. In Italy, aperitivo culture isn't about rushing through a drink—it's about savoring the moment, enjoying the company, and letting the world slow down for a while. Even in our own traditions, patience plays a role. Farmers wait for crops to grow. Bakers let dough rise. Musicians practice for years before they master a song. Waiting isn't wasted time—it's time that adds value.

We didn't kill patience, but we did put it on the endangered list. In our race toward instant everything, we forgot that waiting isn't just about passing time—it's about developing the grit to handle what time throws at us.

Take away waiting, and even minor inconveniences feel catastrophic. Wi-Fi goes out for ten minutes, and people act like civilization has crumbled. If patience is a muscle, a no-wait society leaves us woefully out of shape.

Waiting: It's Not a Bug, It's a Feature

If we can't eliminate waiting entirely, maybe the real challenge is learning to make it meaningful. Instead of treating it like a punishment, we can reclaim it as an opportunity. Maybe waiting isn't just an inconvenience—it's a moment to pause, reset, and appreciate the world around us.

A society that values fairness should aim for balance—reducing unnecessary delays while ensuring that convenience isn't just a privilege for the few. And if we're going to build a future where waiting still exists, we should make sure it's worth the wait.

Optimized Society? No Thanks. We're Delightfully Inefficient.

The real reason waiting will never go away? People. Beautifully, frustratingly, people.

And honestly, would we really want it any other way? Sure, we could live in a hyper-efficient world where everyone moves with robotic precision, never hesitates, never forgets, never holds up the line debating whether they *really* want fries—but what kind of dystopian nightmare would that be?

For all our faults, our quirks and imperfections are what make life interesting. A perfectly optimized society might run smoother, but it sure as hell wouldn't be as fun.

Conclusion: The Line Never Really Ends

If time is a river, waiting is the reflection staring back at us—showing how we handle life's slow currents. We may shrink lines, digitize queues, and optimize every second, but waiting will always find a way back into our lives. And maybe that's not a bad thing.

Because in the end, life isn't just about getting there faster. It's about the moments in between—the pauses, the anticipation, the journey itself.

So the next time you're stuck in line, take a breath. You're part of something bigger. The world may be moving fast, but sometimes, the wait is exactly where you're meant to be.

The Line Is Dead. Long Live the Line

Are we doomed to wait forever? Perhaps. But the better question is: how do we make waiting something worth experiencing? In the final chapter, we explore whether waiting—our universal pastime of scrolling, sighing, and checking the clock—can be transformed into something more. If we're going to spend so much of our lives waiting, we might as well get good at it.

Chapter Sixteen

The Waiting Was the Living

"Every little thing is gonna be alright." —Bob Marley & The Wailers, Three Little Birds
(Even the longest waits end eventually. And sometimes, what's waiting for you is better than you imagined.)

In a world obsessed with speed, what if we treated waiting as a skill instead of a nuisance? Instead of gritting our teeth through delays, we could use those moments to pause, reflect, and maybe even grow. What if waiting wasn't just something to endure—but something to embrace?

Your wise old grandfather (the kind who definitely walked uphill both ways to school) would probably tell you that waiting builds character. And while you might roll your eyes, there's truth in that. Waiting forces us to sit in the space between desire and fulfillment, between *not yet* and *finally*. And in that space, something important happens—we learn patience. We learn presence. We learn that life isn't just a series of arrivals, but a collection of moments in between.

Change your Have To's to Get To's

There's a simple but profound idea that can change the way we experience waiting—and life in general. It comes from Brianna Wiest's *101 Essays That Will Change the Way You Think*, and it's as simple as shifting one word: change your *have to's* into *get to's*.

It's easy to see daily obligations as drudgery. *I have to commute to work. I have to make dinner. I have to wait in this long line.* But what happens when we flip the script? *I get to commute to work*—because I have a job that supports me. *I get to make dinner*—because I have food to nourish myself and the people I love. *I get to wait in this line*—because I can afford the thing I'm waiting for.

That tiny shift reframes everything. Responsibilities become privileges. Annoyances become opportunities. Waiting, instead of being a test of patience, becomes a moment to pause and reflect with gratitude on what we already have. And isn't that what waiting really is? A space between one thing and the next, a chance to breathe, to look around, to remember that at some point, the job, the home, the family, the stability—were all things we once deeply wanted.

It's either that or we keep muttering *this is ridiculous* while rage-refreshing a tracking page. Your call.

Of course, shifting your mindset isn't always easy—especially when you're stuck in traffic, trapped in a DMV line, or constantly checking your email for a long-awaited response. It's one thing to wax poetic about patience; it's another to practice it when you're watching your Uber driver take a scenic detour through the wrong side of town.

But what if, instead of letting frustration take over, you found something else to focus on? Next time you're crawling along in rush-hour traffic, instead of mentally drafting a strongly worded letter to city planners, try naming three things you're grateful for in that moment. Even if it's as basic as, *I have air conditioning. At least I'm not Gaius right now. Hey, Dax and Monica thank you, Armchair Expert rules.*

Or take a checkout line that refuses to move. The natural instinct is to whip out your phone and doomscroll your way through the wait, but what if you didn't? What if, just for a moment, you looked up? Maybe you notice a kid in the cart ahead of you making a ridiculous face. Maybe you overhear an oddly fascinating conversation between two strangers. Maybe, for the first time in weeks, you just let yourself exist in a moment without filling it with digital noise.

And then there's the big stuff—the waits that stretch for weeks or months. The job offer. The medical results. The big life change you're desperate to see unfold. These waits feel the longest because they matter the most. But what if you stopped seeing them as dead space and started seeing them as part of the experience? A trip you wait months for is more exciting than one you book last-minute. A meal you cook slowly tastes better than fast food. The things we anticipate the longest are often the things we appreciate the most.

We can't always control how long we wait, but we *can* control how we experience it. Waiting doesn't have to be a passive, teeth-gritting exercise. It can be a choice—a moment to shift, to notice, to be present. It doesn't have to be wasted time. It can just be time.

The Space Between What Was and What Will Be

Waiting is a strange place. It's not quite the past, not quite the future—a liminal space where life is still unfolding. And what we do in that space matters.

Maybe this is where we learn to let *now* be enough. To stop seeing life as a series of destinations and start recognizing the depth of what's in front of us. Brianna Wiest puts it poetically:

> *"Because it's a succession of 'nows' that will add up, lifting us from awareness of one experience to another, that will be all we have in the end. So what we see in*

> *the experience is what we have to appreciate before we're lifted away from the monotonous routine, because the alternative is that we cease to exist."*

Maybe that's the secret we've been missing all along—that waiting isn't wasted time. It's a reminder to stop clinging to what's next and to fully step into *now*. As Wiest so perfectly writes:

> *"Maybe it is about diving into the deep end and letting now be more than just enough. Realizing that things are only ever as boring and mundane as we let them be. That there are mysteries and experiences and fascinatingly foreign parts of life that we won't see until we take a step out on the wild side, the side of us that isn't concerned about tomorrow."*

You can almost see Simone Weil with a tear in her eye, smiling down at Brianna, nodding in agreement, as if to say, *Finally, someone gets me.* Maybe that's what waiting has been trying to teach us all along—not merely how to endure time, but how to live in it. How to see the magic tucked into the moments we're so quick to dismiss. They unfold in the quiet moments—in the real-time space between what was and what will be.

A few months ago, I downloaded an app that identifies birds by their songs. I expected a neat little gimmick—maybe something to settle a debate over whether that was actually a woodpecker or just a particularly aggressive squirrel. But what I didn't expect was how much it would change the way I experience a walk in the woods.

One morning on the nature trail behind my house, I paused on the trail, let the app listen, and suddenly, my screen lit up: *Black-throated Blue Warbler.* I'd never even heard of it. But there it was, the prettiest blue and black little bird singing his sweet little zee zee zee zoo in the canopy above me—a bird I would have completely ignored if not for that tiny digital nudge.

From that moment on, my hikes weren't just about moving from point A to point B. I started listening—really listening. I noticed the layers of sound, the different calls overlapping like an unscripted symphony. Birds I'd never seen, but now knew by name, were out there, filling the air with music.

It made me wonder: *What else had I been walking past my whole life?*

Because maybe that's the thing about waiting, about stillness—it's not empty. It's full of things we're just not paying attention to. They unfold in these quiet moments—in the now, we just need to pay attention. And once you start looking—really looking—it's incredible what you begin to notice.

Good Things Come to Those Who Wait (And Science Says So)

There's something magical about looking forward to something. Remember the excitement of waiting for your birthday as a kid? The slow build-up of counting down the days, the anticipation of cake, presents, and the sheer joy of a day that was *yours*?

I had to relearn this lesson the hard way. Years ago, I was waiting to hear back about a career-changing opportunity, and every day not knowing the outcome felt like torture. I checked my email obsessively, convinced that refreshing my inbox might somehow force an answer to appear. It didn't. All it did was make me more anxious.

Finally, I gave up. Not in a defeated way, but in a "let me get on with my life" way. I took long walks. I read books that had nothing to do with my career. I forced myself to focus on the present instead of the unknown. And wouldn't you know it—when the news finally came, it was great. But more importantly, I hadn't spent those weeks in misery. I had actually lived in them.

Waiting doesn't have to steal your joy. You just have to stop giving it permission.

That feeling doesn't have to disappear just because we're adults. Anticipation—waiting for something wonderful—actually enhances our enjoyment of it. Studies have shown that the buildup to an event is often as pleasurable, if not more so, than the event itself. Half the fun of a trip, a holiday, or a long-overdue dinner with a loved one isn't just the experience—it's the thrill of counting down to it, imagining what's to come, and letting excitement build.

The ability to wait used to be part of life's rhythm, but modern convenience has rewritten the script. We no longer build anticipation—we bypass it. We're so used to getting what we want immediately—next-day delivery, instant downloads, binge-watching entire seasons—that we've forgotten how good it feels to *look forward* to something. The slow build of anticipation, the delicious sense of something wonderful on the horizon, is a pleasure we rarely allow ourselves anymore.

But what if we did? What if we let waiting work its quiet magic, stretching and deepening our joy instead of rushing to the finish line? What if, instead of rushing to the end, we allowed ourselves to revel in the in-between—the countdown before a long-awaited trip, the growing excitement of a birthday around the corner, the quiet thrill of knowing something wonderful is coming but not quite yet?

We don't just lose time when we eliminate waiting—we lose the sweetness of expectation. The buildup before a concert, the slow unraveling of a story, the quiet pleasure of watching something unfold piece by piece. What if we let ourselves enjoy the wait a little more? What if, instead of trying to eliminate anticipation, we stretched it out like a song we don't want to end?

You'll Enjoy This Section More If You Read It Slowly

This brings us to our old friend *dopamine*. Dr. Anna Lembke, in her book *Dopamine Nation*, explains that our brains are wired to seek pleasure and avoid pain, which is why we crave instant gratification.

Now, let's be real: not all waiting is some profound, life-enhancing experience. Some of it is just plain awful. Waiting for test results or medical diagnosis? Stressful. Waiting to hear back after a job interview? Torture. Waiting for your Uber while watching it drive in the wrong direction? Infuriating.

There's no sugarcoating the fact that some waits are emotionally taxing, even agonizing. The trick isn't to force a smile through gritted teeth—it's to recognize that patience doesn't mean pretending waiting is fun. It means learning to sit with uncertainty without letting it consume you.

Because whether you dread the wait or embrace it, the time will pass either way.

That hit of dopamine we get from checking our phones, ordering two-day shipping, or streaming an entire season in one sitting? It feels amazing—until it doesn't. Because the more we indulge in immediate rewards, the more we dull our ability to enjoy life's deeper, slower pleasures.

This is why waiting—the thing we resist so fiercely—is actually good for us. It strengthens our ability to sit with discomfort, to let anticipation build, to savor something before it arrives.

Think about how much better a meal tastes when you've been looking forward to it. How much sweeter a long-awaited reunion feels. How much more satisfying it is to earn something rather than have it handed to you.

Your grandfather didn't know about dopamine, but he did know this: anything truly worth having is worth waiting for. A good stew. A great novel. A real friendship. The kind of love that lasts. He knew in his core that life's greatest gifts are not always found in the destination but reveal themselves in the journey. Because slowing down isn't just about savoring the moment—it's about reclaiming the kind of life that doesn't always need to be sped up in the first place.

The Grace of a Slower Life

We live in a world that worships efficiency. We order groceries with a swipe. We refresh tracking pages like it'll make the package arrive faster. We honk at red lights like the universe will take that as a suggestion.

But there's another way to live—a slower, more intentional way. The slow living movement is a rebellion against the relentless rush. It's about reclaiming time, savoring small moments, and understanding that not everything needs to be maximized for productivity.

A morning commute doesn't have to be wasted time—it can be a chance to listen to a great podcast, or better yet, to sit in silence and let your thoughts wander. A delayed flight might be the perfect excuse to people-watch and imagine where everyone else is going. A long wait at a restaurant? A chance to be fully present with the person across from you, instead of checking your phone every five seconds.

What if we stopped seeing waiting as an inconvenience and started seeing it as an opportunity?

The Waiting Was the Living

Waiting isn't going away. But what if we stopped

treating it like a problem to be solved and started seeing it as a part of life to be lived?

Because here's a secret no one tells you when you're young: some of life's best moments happen when nothing is happening at all. The conversations you have in long lines. The thoughts that bubble up when you're stuck in traffic. The deep breath you take before something big happens. This is where life happens. In the in-between. We spend so much of our lives chasing finish lines—counting down, crossing off, rushing forward—so certain that happiness lives somewhere just ahead. But what if the real magic isn't in the arrival, but in the unfolding? What if life isn't a race to be won, but a road to be wandered, full of unexpected stops, quiet moments, and turns we never saw coming?

Because waiting isn't just time slipping through an hourglass—it's what fills the glass in the first place. A quiet glance in a waiting room that led to a conversation, that led to a spark, that led to meeting the love of your life. A delayed flight that introduced you to a stranger who became a close friend. A missed train that rerouted your day just enough to reveal something unexpected—like discovering your favorite hole-in-the-wall bookstore you wouldn't have found otherwise. Or a street performer playing so beautifully it made you stop dead in your tracks, a moment captured poetically by Joni Mitchell in *For Free*, reminding us that some of the most breathtaking experiences in life cost nothing at all.

That unseen musician, pouring his heart into the air while the world rushes past, feels more relevant today than ever. In an era where our attention is pulled in a thousand directions, where algorithms decide what we hear and who gets noticed, how many breathtaking moments do we pass by simply because they're not trending?

That street performer still exists. Maybe he's playing saxophone in a subway station, or strumming a guitar on a quiet street corner. Maybe she's singing with a voice so pure it demands to be heard—if only you let it. But most people, ear buds in, eyes locked on their screens, don't even hear the music. They don't look up.

Joni's song was about a missed connection, a fleeting encounter that lingered in her mind long after the moment had passed. And that's the power of waiting, of stillness, of simply noticing. That musician was playing real good for free—but the real question is: are we listening?

The truth is, we are always on our way to something. But if we're too focused on getting there, we'll miss the beauty of being here.

History proves it: some of the greatest ideas in the world weren't born in moments of action, but in moments of waiting. Albert Einstein wasn't in a high-tech lab when he dreamed up the theory of relativity—he was working at a patent office, lost in thought, staring out a window. J.K. Rowling wasn't furiously typing when Harry Potter came to life—she was stuck on a delayed train, letting her mind wander. Sir Isaac Newton wasn't in a classroom when he began to understand gravity—he was simply sitting under a tree, watching apples fall.

The moments we spend waiting aren't empty—they are fertile ground. They are where imagination stirs, where ideas take root, where the mind is free to wander into unexpected brilliance. We spend so much of our lives trying to fill every gap, every silence, every pause. But what if we left a little space? What if, instead of rushing to the next thing, we let the waiting work on us?

Because sometimes, the best things don't happen when we're moving forward. They happen in the stillness, in the pause, in the in-between.

The next time you're caught in a moment of waiting—between where you are and where you want to be—let it hold you. Breathe it in. Let it remind you that life isn't a race from one destination to the next, but a series of pauses, heartbeats, and unfolding moments.

Because one day, you'll look back and realize: the waiting *was* the living.

Acknowledgments

A huge thank you to my editor, William Reilly, for his excellent suggestions and keen editorial eye, Your feedback was invaluable, and this book is sharper, funnier, and all-around better because of you. I'm incredibly grateful! I would also like to thank Acacia W. for her insightful beta reading.

I owe a debt of gratitude to Chris Era, my extraordinary book cover designer. Chris is not only a brilliant creative talent but also a joy to collaborate with.

Brianna Wiest's *101 Essays That Will Change the Way You Think* and Anna Lembke's *Dopamine Nation* were both instrumental in shaping my perspective on waiting—not just as an inconvenience, but as something deeply tied to how we seek pleasure, purpose, and meaning. Their insights made me think, rethink, and, at times, completely change my approach to this book.

Yuval Noah Harari's *Nexus* pushed me to think beyond just efficiency and inconvenience, challenging me to consider how technology, AI, and automation are reshaping not only how we wait, but what it means to be human. His work is a must-read for anyone who wants to dig deeper into the future of agency, choice, and connection in an increasingly automated world.

Oliver Burkeman's *Four Thousand Weeks* was another game-changer—a reminder that time management isn't about squeezing more in, but about making peace with the fact that we can't do it all. His work reinforced the idea that waiting isn't just something to endure—it's an unavoidable part of our too-short, beautifully finite existence.

Endless gratitude to Joni Mitchell, whose music continues to resonate just as powerfully today as it ever has. Her songs are more than melodies—they are maps of the human soul, guiding us through love, loss, wonder, and waiting. *For Free* and so many others remind us to slow down, to listen, to notice. To the next generation: dig deep into her catalog. There's a whole world waiting for you there.

A shoutout to my son, TJ, for suggesting the parable of the cloudy water—such a beautiful and fitting addition to the theme of this book.

A special thanks to my good friend Ramu, who introduced me to the incredible world of Mumbai's Dabbawalas—the nearly flawless lunchbox delivery network that makes our so-called "efficient" systems look like absolute chaos in comparison. Their story is a masterclass in patience, precision, and what's possible when human ingenuity meets a little bit of trust.

To my dear friend Tom, who shared some of the most unforgettable years of my life during my Air

Force days—roommates, wingmen, and partners in mischief. If anyone ever truly learned the meaning of *hurry up and wait*, it was us. Though time and distance have taken us down different paths, true friendship never fades. You remain in my thoughts and heart always.

To the hardworking folks at the DMV and TSA—yes, I poked fun at the long lines, the confusing forms, and the twilight zone of security checkpoints, but please know it comes from a place of deep respect (and, okay, maybe a little trauma). The truth is, you do a tough, often thankless job, with patience, professionalism, and—let's be honest, a level of endurance most of us could never muster. I salute you. Thank you for what you do.

Peace and Love. Embrace the pause, y'all!

Rick Brown spends his days in the world of tech, analyzing customer complaints—many of which, unsurprisingly, involve the agony of waiting. Whether it's navigating data or sitting in a standstill on the highway, he's logged enough hours in life's holding patterns to qualify for some kind of honorary degree.

When he's not knee-deep in algorithms, Rick is drawn to the slow spots in life—the moments in between, where time stretches and unexpected connections are made. *Waiting... In the Age of Instant Everything* is his second book, a natural continuation of the themes explored in his novel, Call Me Al, which examined our need for connection in this age of miracle and wonder. And now, Let's Go Cubbies!

www.ingramcontent.com/pod-product-compliance
Lightning Source LLC
Chambersburg PA
CBHW060452030426
42337CB00015B/1559